Castings:
The Creation Of Sacred Space

By Ivo Domínguez, Jr.
Panpipe

SapFire
Georgetown, Delaware

Published by

SapFire Productions, Inc.
RR 2, Box 511-G (Rt 565)
Georgetown, DE 19947, USA
(302) 855-0699
SapFireInc@aol.com

Illustrations and layout by Ivo Domínguez, Jr. - Panpipe

Castings is the first book in the Wheel of Trees series

Note: You are responsible for your actions. Neither the author nor the publisher are liable for your use of the rituals and methods presented in this book .

ISBN 0-9654198-0-0

Printed and Bound in the United States

Acknowledgements
&
Dedications

This book is dedicated to my beloved James Conrad Welch; to Sue (Brenda) Clauss, James Eric Dickinson, Michael Glen Smith, and Nancy Gail Stewart, my fellows at Seelie Court; and to all my kith in The Assembly Of The Sacred Wheel. I would like to thank them for their support, encouragements, and intellectual stimulation. Their openness to experimentation and to the refinement of vision into manifestation is without peer.

I would also like to acknowledge the influence in my life of the teachings and deeds of Scott Cunningham, the Farrars, Gerald Gardner, Murry Hope, Dolores Ashcroft-Nowicki, Shakmah Winddrum, Starhawk, and Roger Zelazny.

Table Of Contents

Introduction

Castings: The Creation Of Sacred Space is meant to provide a safe and sane introduction to the knowledge and techniques needed to embark upon journeys into magick. The first half of the book supplies some philosophical and theoretical underpinnings in order to make the castings offered in the second half of the book accessible and effective. Hopefully, a balance between theory and practice has been struck that will encourage the development of both understanding and proficiency in the creation of sacred and magickal space. You may wish to try the various castings as you read the book, but I recommend that you finish the book before attempting them. Those items that are marked as exercises should be done as you encounter them.

For the purposes of this book the word *casting* when used as a noun will be taken to mean:

A set of actions, involving a combination of mental, emotional, spiritual, and potentially physical operations, intended to create a volume of space wherein for a certain period of time there is a subjective and/or objective difference from the prevailing baseline of markers for mundane reality.

To *cast* will be used as a verb expressing:

The implementation or the enactment of the set of actions required to bring about a desired, specific, change in the conditions of subjective and/or objective reality of a specific volume of space for a specific duration.

This book explores a number of approaches to the creation, delineation, and understanding of ritual that opens the way to sacred space. The entry into sacred space is one of the most direct routes that leads to the fountainhead of spiritual and metaphysical experience. For most of us, the thrill of the experience that called us to our paths is marked by crossing the borderline into a wider universe. When you took your first step onto your path of magickal and spiritual development did you not long for the strange skies of the otherworlds, conversations with the Shining Ones, keys to the gates, or the smell of flowers in a Faerie glade. Many paths lead to magick and to the experience of sacred space, but the use of castings to cross the threshold into higher realities is one of the most powerful and direct ways to achieve this aim. Encounters with higher realities occur within the matrix of culture and belief. Culture and belief are the foundation of the techniques to reach higher realities[1]. The differences and similarities between magickal systems and Traditions may be thought of as cultural differences. Although culture surely frames the field of experience it is the context of the individual's life that shapes the flow that arises from the fountainhead of spiritual reality. It is my hope that seekers on different paths will be stimulated by the similarities, and the differences between the many traditions leading to sacred space.

For those readers who take a humanistic or a secular approach to integration or actualization, I suggest that you read the word sacred in this book to mean those things that are enduring, worthy of your respect, and of your veneration. As to magick, Aleister Crowley defined magick (spelled with a k to differentiate it from stage magic or trickery) as "the Science and Art of causing Change to occur in conformity to Will."[2] You may read this definition in either physical, psychological and/or metaphysical terms without losing the essence of its meaning. You are encouraged to re-vision the techniques and castings in this book to suit your particular slant or worldview. If you like, consider the material presented in this book as art, theater, and folklore to broaden your poetic insight and imagery of your deeper self.

The paradigm of the Circle and the Quarters is common to many traditions, cultures, and esoteric disciplines; accordingly a good part of this book is devoted to their use and symbolism. In addition to the Circle and the Quarters, other modes of casting sacred space and magickal space will be taught. Whenever possible, instructions will be presented to allow for the use of the *castings* by individuals or by groups. The enactment, experience, and effect of castings is different when done solo as opposed to collectively. You should not consider yourself proficient (all other things considered) in a particular casting until you've used it as an individual and in a group numerous times.

For the most part the chapters stand alone, and may be read out of sequence, but you may gain a better understanding of the castings if you read the chapters in their natural order. The distinctiveness of the castings will become clearer once all the chapters have been read, because it will be possible to compare and contrast their various characteristics. As is true for most writings on esoteric matters, you will gain a deeper or a broader set of in-

---

[1]   By higher I mean more encompassing realities that enclose the lower ones in the manner of the microcosm/macrocosm principle.

[2]   Aleister Crowley, Magick (York Beach, Maine, Samuel Weiser, Inc. 1974) p. 130

sights and awarenesses with repeated readings and with actual practice and experience of the castings. Also many of the nuances of the castings will escape your understanding until you actually use them for specific purposes rather than as exercises.

To help you develop your competency with these castings, I have used the same structural outline in each of the chapters that describes a specific casting. This arrangement should make it easier to learn each of the castings and has the benefit of allowing logical comparisons between the castings' protocols. Watch for the following headings in the instructional chapters as they are the core framework you may use to build your knowledge.

Introduction
The Calling
The Dismissal
Its Qualities And Uses
Principles And Basis For Action
Limitations And Precautions
Interactions With Other Castings Or Magicks
Recommendations For Mastering Its Use
Conclusion

A one page summary of the protocol for each of the castings is available in the appendices. I have found that reducing tension, frustration, and anxiety are essential to effective ritual. I encourage you to use these as aides to mastering the castings. Either take the book with you into your ritual space or photocopy the one page summary. In the long run most people prefer to memorize castings, but in the short run a piece of paper can provide a useful boost to your confidence. You may also wish to enlarge selected diagrams as props for the visualizations that accompany most of the castings.

A number of the castings in this book do not appear in any other written or traditional sources; to the best of my knowledge they are unique. They were created, or more accurately re-created, from my past-life memories, visions, and careful thought based on this life's learning. These castings have been in use for over twelve years by the coven[3] I helped to found, and for several years by the other covens in my Tradition. I will not burden you with my past-life stories as to the origins of these castings, as I believe that such memories and visions should be taken with a grain of salt. I will say that the visions that led to these castings have been grounded in the reality of practical use, and that I feel secure in recommending their use. I have tested the

---

[3] This coven is Keepers of the Holly Chalice a part of The Assembly of the Sacred Wheel a legally recognised Wiccan religious organization.

limits of these castings and taken personal risks in order to assure their safety and efficacy. They have also been successfully used by individuals and groups outside my Tradition which suggests that these castings are adaptable.

As you are reading this book, if you find a reference to an unfamiliar concept, word or magickal system you may wish to jot it down in your journal as a reminder to look it up later. There is also a suggested reading list at the back of this book that may be of use to you. You will notice that I am assuming that you *are* keeping a journal. For some people keeping a journal is a pleasant diversion— for many others it is drudgery. Don't put off keeping a magickal journal because of your preconceptions about what such a journal should be like; it need not be bound in tooled leather nor does it require the best prose or penmanship. Whether your journal is a note pad, a file on a computer, or a handmade book, it can serve you well. The purpose of a magickal journal[4] is to assist you in keeping track of your experiences, observations, and questions so that you may further your efforts on the path. Above and beyond the forgetfulness that is normal, there is often an inner or an outer resistance to change and growth that often expresses itself as a forgetting of just those things that we need most to progress spiritually. Magickal journals are one of our best shields against forgetfulness and lethargy, perhaps second-best only to participation in a healthy working group.

I also recommend that you seek out a working group, knowing as I make that recommendation just how hard it is to find an appropriate group. Don't rush into joining a group. Make a fully informed choice whenever joining a group because the act of joining is magick that puts many changes in motion. If for whatever reasons you find that you cannot connect with a formally organized magickal working group, you may wish to seek out a study group or form one. There are many pitfalls associated with study groups, but it is far better to be in a study group than to conform to a magickal working group that does not fit your temperament and beliefs.

Lastly, it's alright to be overwhelmed; even virtuoso pianists began with simple finger exercises. Don't take that example as an exhortation to become a virtuoso— your goal may not be to become a virtuoso. There are many who play well enough to bring themselves and their fellows joy, and that is enough. As you work your way through *Castings: The Creation Of Sacred Space* listen for inner guidance in whatever way that you practice. If you feel comfortable in doing so, you may ask the help of the Spirit of the Birch tree. The impetus to write this book came after a contact that I had with the Birch Deva[5] . Birch is the first tree in the Celtic Tree Calendar that marks the thir-

---

4   These may be referred to by a variety of names. In my Tradition, The Assembly of the Sacred Wheel, it is called a Book of Lights & Shadows.

5   A deva, in this usage, is the oversoul or groupmind of a particular species.

teen Lunar months and the Sun's five stations of the year. Birch is *Beth* , the first letter in the Celtic Tree Alphabet. Birch is the setter of boundaries, it was the tree that marked the boundary between the green Earth and the melting glaciers at the end of the last Ice Age. It is the tree of inception and stands at the beginning of things. The setting of sacred bounds and castings which are the beginning of magick are under the rule of Birch. This book is upheld by the essence of the Birch. Invoke the wisdom of the Birch as you work through this book.

❋2❋

Your Vision

Although many different methods will be presented in subsequent chapters, often with somewhat technical explanations, I would like to underscore that magick and ceremony are arts not sciences. What you accomplish using the various castings is not only dependent upon your intellectual understanding, but your passion, creativity, and vision. The whole of what you believe is the foundation of all your castings. In certain branches of the Western Magickal Tradition students are asked to a create a pantacle[1], a disk marked with symbols to form a visual representation of their personal concept of the universe. The pantacle is then used in ritual as a reminder or a focus of that integrated vision. The process of taking all they know or believe and concentrating it into an image is a powerful learning experience. You may wish to undertake the task of creating a pantacle or choose another method for distilling your knowledge into essence. You may wish to write a poem or a story to accomplish the same end. You may wish to paint your vision or to create a richly detailed image in your mind's eye if your hand is not suited to the visual arts. You may wish to make a ritual garb adorned in a way that shows your relationship to your vision. Regardless of how you approach this task, it is a work of art.

The development of a personal vision, style, or voice, in the arts is a difficult undertaking. When it comes to the creation of a personal vision that encompasses the sacred, the quest is all the more strenuous because it must express the fullness of your being. A part of that search may include explorations in philosophy, mythology, and metaphysics. Perhaps the most overlooked and yet one of the most central parts of any vision or worldview is a model of or paradigm for the nature of Divinity. The meaning of sacred space and the relationship of the person creating the space to their concept of Deity has countless ramifications. One thing that I hold as true for all paths is that it is always advisable to acknowledge the presence and power of the Divine whenever a casting is performed. A work-plan for the development of a coherent personal vision of castings is beyond the scope of this

---

[1] The pantacle is also called a pentacle but that can create confusion with the five pointed star that is common to many systems of magick.

book, but I do recommend that you consider the difference between what you *think* and what you *believe* as an essential part of your spiritual development.

Exercise

Write three short myths: one should describe the creation of the manifest universe; another the creation of humans; and the last a meeting between humans and your concept of the Divine. A week or two after you have written the three myths, read them again and look for any resonances between the myths and your concept of sacred space. Write new myths every few months and repeat the process for new insights on the state of your beliefs. This exercise is as simple and as difficult as it sounds.

The Circle Is The Beginning Of Magick: A Personal Vision

As a way to communicate what I mean by a coherent personal vision of castings, I offer my personal vision on the deeper meanings inherent in the casting of a circle as a point of departure for the quest for your own visions.

The basic unity of creation is held as a primal truth in many spiritual paths. This unity does not imply uniformity, it implies multiplicity connected through a commonality of source, of foundations of existence, and in some philosophies a commonality of purpose. This underlying unity of the great diversity of the Universe allows for a host of Goddesses and Gods that are each one with the whole. The word *Universe* (with the same root as the word unity) encompasses all of space, time, and everything that exists, seen and unseen. In Wicca, as in Native American traditions, all of space and time is held as sacred. The Universe is seen as divinity manifest, and in Wicca is the body of the Goddess. Within this perspective, the Universe is sacred, therefore every and all of its parts are sacred. The beauty and glory of this perspective of the Universe is one of the roots of the spiritual desire to experience it as a unity.

To truly experience the whole of one's self is a tall order, to experience the wholeness of the Earth, or larger yet— our arm of the Galaxy is unimaginable. For humans the capacity for ecstatic union with the totality of things is generally achieved only after soul refining work, and then only for brief periods. In some traditions this is seen as a human failing, but in an Earth Religion like Wicca this need is seen as natural and reflective of our nature as incarnate beings. This is no more a failing than a cell acknowledging that it is a part of an organ within an organism, but it should also be acknowledged that each cell carries the pattern in its DNA of the whole organism. There is no shame in physical beings abiding by the laws of physical existence, let alone the limits of psychology and personality. There is also the recognition that the fullness of experience is on a continuum, perhaps several continua.

Communion with the Universe while incarnate is much like trying to reach the speed of light while in the physical level of the Universe. As you approach the speed of light, Einstein taught that your rate of time slows down, and your mass increases until at the speed of light time stops and mass is infinite. The faster you go the heavier the load becomes, and the less time you have to push. It would take infinite energy to reach the speed of light whereupon time would cease to pass, and your mass would be infinite. Using this as a metaphor for attempts at ecstatic union, it would take infinite consciousness to reach total communion with the Universe. Having met these conditions, you would meet the criteria that many hold true for Deities. This imagery may seem a bit extreme, but it underlines a very important point: the effective creation of magickal space revolves around adherence to the patterns of physical, metaphysical, and psychological laws.

The casting of a Circle is an acknowledgement of the limits of human consciousness, and is a tool to reach beyond those limits by choosing specific boundaries and limits. There is a basic human need for division, and segmentation in consciousness. Our concentration, attention, and rates of information processing are limited. Our limits call forth the necessity for the selection of different modes of awareness for different purposes. When we read our attention is focused on the message carried by the words — not the slight irregularities in the shapes of the letters caused by the ink spreading into the fibers of the paper. When we dream, certain gates are open to us, but the tools of rational thought are normally confiscated at these gates. Humans are tool users, and consciousness was our first tool, not a chipped flint. Although many are versatile, no one tool is applicable for every situation — the same is true for consciousness. Castings and different modes of consciousness are among the tools, when used with proficiency, that allow us to build and to travel our path to the Universe.

The casting of a Circle is also an opportunity to affirm the parts of yourself that exist outside of the physical frame of reference. It is an opportunity to co-create and to recreate yourself and your universe in conjunction with whatever name(s) you give to Deity force(s) of immanence and transcendence. It is a way to make easier the shift from the consciousness used to function in daily life to the consciousness used in connecting with Life in the greater sense. A Circle is an attempt at reconciliation between between personal, collective, and transpersonal realities.

Castings are the inception of Magick and the creation of intentional paradox. The intent of casting a Circle is, in part, to scale the Universe down to the range of human consciousness. The creation of any division or subsetting of the Universe in any way produces paradoxes. The paradox of the representation of the infinite, the macrocosm, in the terms of the finite, the microcosm, is an unending source of power and inspiration. The old Hermetic idea of the microcosm within the macrocosm is interwoven into many esoteric traditions. It is often expressed in this way: "As Above So Below, But In Another Manner." The simplicity of this axiom can be deceptive. Current Western culture tends to overvalue those things that are sophisticated on the surface, transparent in their workings, and measurable. Poetic truths are often set aside as less important or are trivialized because the concept of *mystery* is suspect. This poetic Hermetic axiom applies across temporal or spatial spans. It is the connecting rainbow bridge between times, places, and differences of scale or vibration, and as such is a harmonizer of the paradoxes produced in the creation of sacred space. The intentional paradox of a magickal casting is a poetic truth that is seemingly self contradictory but coherent. The apparent simplicity of a fertilized egg, a hazel nut, or the moment before the Big Bang are held as similar in their state of beginning by this axiom. Wiccan Magick contains many poetic truths that are great levelers, that bring the sense of peer relationship and responsibility to the colossal and the small. Like the Universe, we began with all of our matter and potentiality in one cell, and we proceeded to split and to expand. Life, in its greater sense of *all that is evolving*, unfolds through the process of specialization, individuation, and harmonious relation to the laws of matter. Viewed in this context, the casting of a circle is an extension of this process.

Many magickal traditions use the Four Sacred Directions and Center as a way to plot a coordinate in space/time. In some ways the casting of a circle is like starting a journey in that one's bearings must be determined before setting course. Unlike mundane navigation that is based on the finite globe, the casting of a Circle is set in all of space and time, and the movement is not through space but through planes of perception and of reality. In Wiccan Magick, the Circle is said to take us between the Worlds, in this statement there are twin paradoxes. In being between the worlds we are in all worlds, and in no worlds. Although we are elsewhere and elsewhen in a Circle, we still stand upon the ground, and in the time wherein the Circle was cast. Even in the end, the *Circle is open but unbroken* because it exists in time, outside of time, and in the heart.

A Quarters-cast Circle in the Wiccan manner is more than a coordinate, a gate to higher planes, and a paradox - it is a model of the poetic vision of the faith. Present in the Circle is the Wheel of the Year and the intertwining of the Solar and Lunar cycles with the life of the Earth. Present in the Circle is the power of the elements, and their manifestations as forces and states, as Slyphs, Salamanders, Undines, and Gnomes, and as the five sacred parts of self: the body, mind, heart, soul, and spirit. Present in the Circle are the chants, the incense, the drums, the dances, and the people that shape, and are shaped by living traditions.

In its fullness, a Circle can contain a richness so complete that if all of Wicca were lost except for the way to cast a Circle, and its symbolism, the faith would renew itself from that one seed. A Quarters-cast Circle has the potential to be a holographic representation of the evolving energy pattern that is the way of Wicca. The same is potentially true of any casting within the context of a tradition.

Do not allow the casting of a Circle to become merely the preliminary step in a magickal working. Consider the profundity and the power of creating sacred space in every Circle. Remember and reconnect with the poetic truths that are the seed of sacred space.

3

Inner Preparations

Of all the variables to consider, the quality of any casting is determined, to the largest part, by the internal state of the person or persons involved in the creation of the space. This is one of the reasons why many systems and traditions of spiritual, magickal, or psychic development place such a high priority on self-knowledge and self-development as prerequisites to accomplishment, and to initiation. Depending upon the person, and the circumstances of their life, the development or the maintenance of the proper internal state may prove difficult. The lack in most people's lives of connection to a community, and to themselves through rites of passage and integration that lead to empowerment make this task difficult. Sorting through the baggage of our up-bringing, and realizing, and correcting our deficits in awareness and experience can be a lengthy and painful process that is never quite complete.

There is a common, futile, temptation to attempt to buy magickal prowess through tools or powerful incantations. This is aggravated by the materialism of Western culture, where the perception of the intrinsic value of people is reduced, and the value of objects is increased. Neither a powerful object, a magical place, nor a potent astrological occurrence can substitute for clarity and strength of mind, heart, and purpose. Some suggest that we are now moving into an Age that we will use the mind alone, without the use of props, for all our castings; I believe this to be an unbalanced reaction against the spiritual/material dichotomy of the Age that we are leaving. There are tools that can magnify the power of a casting, but the degree of their efficacy depends upon the user. If, by chaos or by fate, a person comes by power that outstrips their capacity, or their wisdom to use it, misfortune frequently follows. Tools, physical or non-physical, are useful, indeed are necessary in some cases, and will be discussed later in this book.

Self-development is the basis for magickal training. Even if you are not concerned by admonitions about risks, please consider the benefits that self-development brings to every part of life as reason enough to proceed with a balanced program of magickal training. The process of self-actualization is often slow and arduous, filled with dark nights of the soul, but also bright days as well. It also tends to follow cycles wherein we think we know nothing, then something, then everything, then nothing again. Do not despair that the road seems long, or allow yourself to be trapped in the *tyranny of excellence* . Many people are vexed by the hidden belief that if something is not perfect, or at the very least is not comparable to the work of masters, that it is not worthy. This belief often inhibits development through the imposition of unreasonable standards. If through a mix up, an essay written by a high school student was submitted, by their older sibling, to their college professor, and was graded harshly, most people would think the grade inappropriate. Seen in the light of cycles of growth, it becomes clear that effort, and participation are the true measures of worth. Every stage of development has inherent beauty.

The inner preparation for embarking into sacred space occurs on many levels of which this chapter will explore three in some detail. For the purposes of a casting, the internal state of a person will be regarded as a composite of: their current state of mind, and spirit; their emotional, and physical energy level; and the summation of their knowledge as incorporated into experience. There are many other ways to describe inner preparations; consider these three overlapping divisions as a framework to give order to the information. The planning and design of a ritual may be considered to be like that of a ballet. With knowledge, creativity, and technical expertise the ballet will certainly have a chance of success, but in the end it is the dancers' passion, expressed through skill, that will determine the outcome. Inner preparation for castings is the invocation, and the evocation of that passion and precision. We will return to various aspects of what constitutes inner preparation in subsequent chapters as they apply to specific castings.

State Of Mind And Spirit

In this section mind will refer to memory, cognition, linear thought, and pattern recognition. Spirit will refer to essence, core identity, and your connection to what exists beyond the self.

Background

In planning a ritual or a working, use your mind to select the most appropriate casting for the intended purpose. Analyze the strengths, weaknesses, and virtues of the selected casting in a cognitive way, and then subject it to spiritual scrutiny. The form, and the *essence* of a casting, and an intended purpose must be in harmony. The determination of such a harmony is a matter of mental and spiritual agreement.

The ability to create, and to verify this harmony, and agreement will be the product of mental, and spiritual development. Mental development means learning things, both ideas and information. The view that you don't need to memorize things you just need to know where to look them up may be well, and good for some fields, but it does not work with magick. Much of what is entailed in spiritual development can be equated with integrity. Magickally, spiritual development is also a matter of establishing a *defined* and a *definite* relationship with whatever forces and forms you use to conceptualize your theology and cosmology. This means knowing the details of systems, pantheons, myths, etc., so that when you have visions and awarenesses you will be able to bring the spiritual experience into grounded development. Without the grit provided by concrete details, our wheels spin, and we mire in our efforts to travel beyond the here and now.

Before

The most immediate mental preparation is to have the details, and the order of the casting clearly in mind. Know what you intend to do. When appropriate and possible, memorize as much of the casting as you are able. This is also the time to be certain that any props or tools that may be needed are ready. Spiritual preparation may involve meditation, prayer, affirmation, or any other technique that reaches for a connection between the personal and the transpersonal. Finding personal symbols, that you can visualize, representative of your relationship to your spirituality may make the transition into the proper state of spirit more complete.

During

Mind and spirit's adaptations to the altered reality within a casting can be incompatible. In other words, it is easy to become distracted and disoriented. The planes of reality that the mind touches differ from those that the spirit touches in terms of the rate that time passes, and the forms that information takes. To be effective you must find the places where mind and spirit interlace in the same rhythm. If you find yourself becoming unfocused pay attention to your breathing or your heart beat to return to sharper focus. If this is a persistent problem you may find some assistance by chewing on a fresh Yarrow floret during ritual. Yarrow is an aromatic, bitter herb that helps to clear the psychic palate.

After

The same day as the casting take time to reflect upon how the casting (and the ritual) was executed and how effective it felt. While it is still fresh in mind jot down notes to yourself on what worked, and what didn't work for future reference. Over time as experience is gained, the effect of the current state of mind and spirit holds less sway over the outcome much in the same way that a single grade changes less and less of a cumulative average as more and more course work is completed.

Emotional And Physical Energy

Background

The inner preparation of emotional and physical energy is primarily purification. The term *purification* implies the removable of undesirable elements, an increase in homogeneity, and/or a greater adherence to a pattern or standard. Another layer of meaning in purification is the release of attachments to negative thoughts or the concerns of daily life. In earlier times, preparation typically included seclusion, special diets or fasting, ritual baths, and meditation as a part of purification. Any or all of these methods, that center on emotional and physical energies, may suit your needs or temperament. Bear in mind it is the essence, not the form, that matters in purification; therefore in most cases less elaborate methods will suffice. Purification methods do have their limits. It is not reasonable to assume that you can load up on food, toxins (alcohol, etc.), have an argument, and then have a purification method, however pure its essence, rid you of the forms that will interfere with your work. Entering the casting in, "perfect love and perfect trust" [1] should be the goal. The touchstone for whether or not the emotional purification was successful should be your sense of having your mood altered, clarified, and stabilized. The test for physical energies is your sense of your vitality.

Before

Immediately prior to the casting it is important to put aside all the anxieties and irritations of day to day life. I say *put aside* as opposed to release or dismiss because our troubles are very real to us, and should be treated as valid, worthy of work, and of healing— all of which takes time. *Putting aside* means that the trouble will be neither forgotten nor shunned, rather that it will be returned to its rightful place at the proper time. This distinction is important because it helps to reduce resistance and self-sabotage by treating the shadow part of yourself with respect.

As you probably have already discovered for yourself there are deep, mutual, bonds between the emotions and the body. Provision for one must involve

---

[1] This phrase summarizes the Wiccan ideal of what should be held in the heart when in sacred space. It is primarily about yourself and not what you expect of others.

the other. Attending to your physical well being is an on-going matter that involves exercise, a balanced diet, sexuality, adequate rest, and the avoidance of toxins. There are many equally effective paths that lead to a vital physical self; find a path that suits you. It is easy to neglect or ignore the body while questing for magick, but if the flesh is weak the spirit eventually loses its will, and its home.

It is important to ground and center to allow for a unobstructed flow of energy and intent in a casting. The next chapter covers grounding and centering.

During

Though it is the state of mind and spirit that delineates the shape of a casting; it is the emotional and physical energy that provides the bulk of the power that is needed for success. To generate or liberate the needed energy you must *let go* and *let loose*. If you are thinking that I mean *let go* and *let loose* in a meditative sense of surrendering yourself to the flow of the casting, then you are partially right. The missing piece, that is more important, is the surrender of judgments about how silly, clumsy, awkward, or comical you may appear as you perform the casting. Self-judgments during a working can sap away confidence, resolve, and emotional energy that in turn causes the body to be stiff, the voice to lack force, and the life force to be curtailed in its flow. Stop self-critical thoughts as soon as you sense the thoughts forming. Replace the thoughts with affirmations of your ability and confidence, then proceed.

Magickal work requires a certain amount of comfort with vulnerability. Vulnerability and intimacy are often linked, and magickal work whether undertaken alone or in a group is self-relevatory and intimate. It is a common experience to have activities or circumstances in our lives where we are shy or unassured. Dancing, singing, expressing affection, or expressing our creativity can activate our insecurities— or heal them. These areas that may make us nervous are often things that we deeply want to do or to have. Strong desire often encourages vigorous efforts at overcoming or releasing obstacles on our path. What I recommend to you is that you apply the experiences, and the tools that you have gained in other areas of your life to the question of being comfortable in a magickal setting. Magick is as much a part of life as anything else is.

After

Shortly after leaving the casting take time to consciously take on the troubles and concerns that you had put aside before the casting. This ensures that you choose the manner in which the concerns return to your mind, preventing some unpleasantries. You should ground and center at the end of the working, and later if you still feel an excess or an imbalance. I strongly encourage you to do a careful reading of the chapter on grounding and centering. If during the working there were persistent doubts and self-criticisms you may wish to write them down so that you can deal with them later.

Exercise

Mirror work is one technique to deal with issues of letting go, and being free, and powerful in ritual. Place yourself in front of a mirror and do some of the things that made you feel silly. Make certain that you do not actually do enough to call a casting or interfere with the working that you've recently completed. Watching yourself chant, or wave a wand in the air, or whatever it was that triggered your discomfort is one way to use a mirror to desensitize yourself. End mirror work by looking into your own eyes and speaking a promise or an affirmation to yourself.

Incorporated Knowledge

Background

Examples of incorporated knowledge in action include: driving a car, playing a musical instrument, swimming, or any other skilled activity where many of the operations occur with little apparent conscious control as a part of the undertaking while the mind is very much in control of the purpose and direction of the activity. The word *incorporate* in this sense is true to its Latin roots of: in + corpus (body), in addition to the definition of working something into an existing form to create a new whole, and also the meaning of giving form or embodying something. In keeping with the esoteric teaching that we have many bodies, nested within each other, ranging from pure matter to pure spirit, we should consider the concept of incorporated knowledge as applying to all our bodies. Examples of incorporated knowledge implemented in spiritual terms includes activities such as clairvoyance or channeling.

Incorporated knowledge also attends to the tension of the power exchange between the conscious and the unconscious elements of the self. Carl G. Jung states, "It does not lie in our power to transfer 'disposable' energy at our pleasure to a rationally chosen object." [2] In relation to castings we are very definitely attempting to transfer energy to a rationally chosen object through conscious effort; therefore we must deal with the actuality that our energy, attention, and intent is divided between our various selves, each of which has

---

[2] Carl Gustav Jung, *Two Essays on Analytical Psychology* (London: Bailiere, Tindall, & Cox, 1928) p. 52.

qualitatively different modes of consciousness, each with quantitatively distinct (and variable) shares of our personal power.

Knowledge that has not been brought into this almost instinctual level of use, by repeated practical application, has diminished effect and utility because of resistance, and in some situations counter-efforts between the conscious and the unconscious. If this were the East, incorporated knowledge would be thought of as the artless art of Zen. Herrigel in describing the Zen mode of ink painting said, "The hand that guides the brush has already caught and executed what floated before the mind at the same moment the mind began to form it, and in the end the pupil no longer knows which of the two—mind or hand—was responsible for the work."[3] In the West, like the East, we strive for unity of purpose within the self, but unlike the East we strive for that unity through ever greater levels of patterning leading towards a modeling of the infinite rather than through simplification of the personal self and direct identification with the infinite.

Development

As you've probably gathered, the development of incorporated knowledge comes through persistent and consistent practice. How many methods, actions, or techniques you may effectively work with at the same time to develop incorporated knowledge will vary dramatically from case to case. The nature of the knowledge also plays a significant part in determining what is possible. The more similar the techniques or topics are, the more difficult it becomes to integrate them coherently if they are being incorporated at the same time. Conversely, similarity of nature speeds the process if the topics are approached in sequence. For example: attempting to learn Spanish and Italian at the same time has the potential for considerable confusion, but if you master one of the languages first the second comes quickly and with greater ease. Both number and nature will play a part in setting the pace of your progress.

In approaching every topic, theme, or technique attempt to find ways to engage all your senses, your bodies (physical and otherwise), and the full span of your knowledge in order to fully assimilate the work at hand so that it can be incorporated. In many ways incorporated knowledge is the essence of wisdom.

On page 20 there is a diagram that offers one way to conceptualize the relationships between different parts of the self. Take some time to explore this diagram. We will pick up this theme again later in chapters 7 & 14.

---

[3] Eugen Herrigel, *Zen In The Art Of Archery* (Vintage Books Edition, 1971) p. 46

Higher Consiousness
(Superset, Unitary, Divine/Pranic)

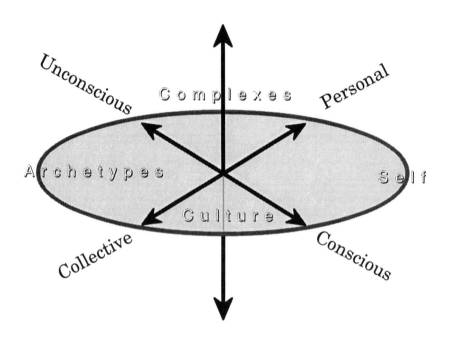

Lower Consiousness
(Subset, Collective, Elemental/Cthonic)

﹌4﹌

Sensing And Making Sense Of Energy

Although it is possible to work with subtle energies in sacred space without a clear or a conscious awareness of these workings the results may be less satisfactory and the experience less satisfying for all those who are involved. It is hard to work if you can't perceive what you're doing. This chapter explores some of the ways that we sense and make sense of psychic impressions. Hopefully the perspectives and ideas presented will help you to make better use of your psychic and magical talents as a whole. However anxious you may be to start working with castings and magick immediately, you may find that the time spent working through this chapter will be well invested.

Be aware that subtle energies are strongly effected by the power of thought. This means that the act of perception also modifies that which you observe and as such is an active process with multiple feedback loops. In learning to better sense and resolve subtle energies you are also learning to manipulate it. As throughout all of this book you are encouraged to pause and to use the exercises suggested as you read.

To begin to open up to our psychic senses we must first be well grounded in our understanding of our physical senses and of their view of the world. What we grasp of the world around us is for the most part an approximation of reality. This approximation is shaped by the physical nature of our sense organs, by the nature of those energies to which our sense organs respond, and by our personal and cultural preferences. This network of filters that results in our perceptions is very complex and as a result of this complexity is only stable in a dynamic fashion. This dynamic stability is much like balancing on one foot, filled with constant corrections and swayed by subtle influences. Despite the implication that the process of perception is far from stable, daily life experience tends to work from the assumption that our senses are one of the few solid foundations of our existence. Much of our sense of security in our reality comes from a trust in the solidity of our senses.

The first step on the path to working with subtle energies is to open your senses to their reality and your mind their perception. Opening to psychic perception can be difficult or threatening for many people because of the fear, whether conscious or unconscious, that if the narrowly defined set of allowable perceptions or senses were altered that on many levels that we would lose our way in the world. This is very understandable for many reasons.

The overwhelming amount of raw sensory data that enters through our skin, eyes, ears, nose, mouth, and other senses if unprocessed would be more like noise than information. We perceive the world by reducing and summarizing our sensory information until it is small enough or compressed enough to fit within the bandwidth of our consciousness and our attention span. Further we choose to attend to the world in terms of what is human and culturally relevant. At equal volumes, the sound of a human voice is easier to grasp than a bird song. At a quick glance two similar human faces can be distinguished but the faces of two cats may seem identical. Cultural expectations of what is real and/or important also determine what we perceive. Eskimos and other Northern dwelling peoples have many words to describe snow whereas most Southerners have only a handful to describe the same phenomena. Lacking these words, though the eyes of humans send roughly the same information to the brain, what would be perceived by the Eskimo and the Southerner is likely to be different. The good news is that we have the capacity to increase the amount of sensory data we can effectively use with practice and patience. Also the broadening of cultural perspectives can broaden the range of what can be not only sensed but what can be perceived.

Sensing

Direct perception and comprehension of subtle energies is difficult and uncommon. Further it is often the case that direct perceptions quickly fade from the mind like dreams, like mist in the sun. Further, they are hard to understand because they lack references to our daily waking existence. Short of the quantum leap of a revelatory experience, the surest route to sensing subtle energies is to use the vehicle of what you already know, and find comfortable. This means using the physical senses that you are already using as metaphors for perceiving what is sensed by your inner senses. Think of your five familiar senses as the circuitry in an esoteric television set that catches elusive subtle waves and makes those inaudible and invisible waves intelligible. Paradoxically, immersing yourself in your physical senses is one of the ways out of them. Further still along the path the distinction between the inner and outer senses is minimized as you become more fully integrated.

The process of integration involves the use of all your senses. In using the exercises in this book or in attempting the castings try to *realize* them rather than visualizing them. A well known magical axiom is that words have power therefore the term visualization must be considered as limiting and inadequate. What you can create within your mind is as real as your capacity to endow the creation with the attributes of sound, weight, smell, and other sensory qualities. To call this merely visualization unconsciously prejudices the experience to be primarily visual. In this book the term *realization* will be used as a more inclusive way of describing this inner process. If you are familiar with pathworking then consider realization a subset of the mental techniques used in pathworking. If you are not familiar with pathworking then call to mind the richness of a vivid dream or of a well written page in a novel you like as measure of the completeness of a well crafted mental experience. In realization the goal is to strive towards realism in the experience.

Because of the wide range of differences between individuals and also within individuals over time, the choices of sensory modalities as metaphors for the subtle energies will vary. In any case continual efforts to use as many of your senses as possible will yield powerful long term results. Persistence results in the *incorporation* of the mechanisms of psychic perception and easy movement in shifting your focus of awareness between different planes of realty. Consider the following explorations of the senses and please try the exercises at the end of this chapter:

Tactile

For many people the sensing of subtle energies as tactile is their first real entry to opening their talents. It is also through touch that people often first cause changes or motion in working with energies. Commonly people will report pressure, temperature changes, tingling, itching, etc. To make the most out of the information relayed through touch you must refresh and broaden your touch vocabulary. Try to realize these sensations: What does a feather feel like drawn across your forearm? How would you describe the sensations of an emery board on your fingernails? What sense of temperature is your finger stuck into a sundae, touching both ice cream and hot fudge? What does it feel like when you have to yawn? Can you name what is different between the itch from a mosquito bite and the itch from a cut that is healing? As you can see this sensory modality can make many fine distinctions.

As part of an opening to the modality of touch you may wish to explore your own body and how touch varies from area to area. In this exploration you will find that this is more that just a question of different levels of sensitivity or insensitivity but is actually a matter of qualitative differences. For example, both the tip of your finger and the tip of your tongue are highly sensitive but if they touch a piece of metal they will register different sensations. A wonderful secondary benefit of these explorations is getting better in touch with your body and increasing your capacity to ground.

Visual

The desire to see auras, chakras, energy, etc. is often intense and the results that people have in seeing subtle energies is often unsatisfactory relative to expectations. Western culture is very visually oriented and people want to see things with "their own eyes" in order to confirm their validity. This desire can lead to trying too hard and perceiving little, with little accuracy. To *see* requires learning, relearning, and unlearning. As babies we learn to see. As children and adolescents we learn to separate imagination from reality and often throw out the baby with the bath water. As adults we need at the very least to unlearn the blinders that pass for waking consciousness. One readily accessible tool to expand your awareness of nuances and color vocabulary is to go to a paint store and pick up a handful of sample strips and spend time looking at the colors. Another way involves using the spectrum cast on a wall by a crystal or a prism. Hold a piece of white paper so that the spectrum is projected onto it and slowly change its angle so that the spectrum becomes stretched. With some care you can fill the paper with one main color at a time so that you can see the gradual progression through the sequence of red, orange, yellow, green, blue, indigo, and violet. If you have some amount of color blindness try working on expanding your capacity to distinguish between the colors that you can see and attempt to *feel* or *hear* the differences in the colors that appear the same to you.

Deaf people, who sign, may find that having their language grounded in signs and motions provides them with additional tools to interpret what they see.

Auditory

Sound is a tool used in many techniques and traditions as a way to alter consciousness and to modulate energy. Singing, chanting, toning, and drumming are among the active approaches to the use of sound, while listening to music or tones is a receptive approach to the use of sound in energy work. This is also the case with psychic work, but you are also encouraged to *sense* energies as sounds and to *project* energies as sounds. One of the primary avenues of communication for hearing people is through spoken languages and music. One byproduct of this focus on sound is a wealth of patterns based in sounds to draw upon in deciphering information derived from psychic senses. Another is that often people can resolve many tracks of information simultaneously in an aural format. Sight generally has a distinct focal point whereas sound tends to have a focal area or plane. Take time to listen to a familiar piece of music. While listening pick out your favorite parts (a voice, an instrument, a melody, etc.) and alternate between listening to the whole and to parts of the music as it plays. How much of the music can you attend to at once?

Taste, Smell, & Other Senses

Although most people will find that their capacity to sense or to work with subtle energies will take form and pattern from touch, sight, and sound there are significant advantages to openness to all the physical senses. Taste and smell analogies for psychic perceptions can convey instinctual reactions in a very crisp and succinct way. Memory or long hidden things can also cause smell or taste sensations. Our senses of balance and motion can describe the flow of energy with great accuracy. Consider also your awareness of senses that are combinations of or a synthesis of senses, for example the sense of rhythm. As with the other sensory modalities that have just been discussed you can create exercises or situations that can awaken and strengthen your sensibilities of taste and smell. You may wish to redo the exercises suggested for tactile sensitivity with an inward focus of attention to work on inner senses.

Resolving

As you become more consciously aware of your psychic senses you will begin to develop new filters to reduce and to refine the incoming data to a manageable amount. You will also begin to assign meaning to what you perceive through your own personal symbolism. This is more than simply a matter of different viewpoints or perspective. As in the drawing of a figure with pastels, psychic perception is a matter of choosing (consciously or unconsciously) what to leave out and how to compress the most meaning into a few streaks of color. In a very real way we are all artists, musicians, and writers in that we all have a different style and aesthetic to bring to bear upon our interpretations of reality. It should come as no surprise that if people's perceptions of physical reality vary widely that our perceptions of subtler realities, having fewer form restrictions than the physical ones, should be even more varied. It is very important to keep this in mind when sharing or comparing psychic perceptions with others. Perceptions should be compared in terms of their meaning not in terms of a literal comparison of symbols or sensations since they were composed to provide a personal meaning for the perceiver.

As important an accomplishment as it may be to clear a channel, and focus and filter psychic perceptions onto the mind's wide screen, Dolby sound, private screening room, the real accomplishment will be when the movie becomes intelligible. It may be interesting to watch foreign art films with subti-

tles in another foreign language just as it may be interesting to see or hear interesting patterns in an aura or in a sacred space, but what does it mean?
Let's use the metaphor of learning a foreign language to explore the development of psychic sensibility. Consider gaining access to your psychic sensations and perceptions to be the learning of the sounds and the shapes of the letters in this new language. Then you begin to learn words. You assign a meaning from your language to describe a pattern in the other language which you know to be a word. With time you learn more words and begin to understand sentences, and with persistence the day comes when you can think or understand this other language without translating it to your native tongue first. In fact one of the true signs of mastery of another language is when you begin to dream in the other language. This metaphor can be stretched further still in that psychic perceptions can resemble lucid dreaming, dreaming with a hand at the rudder on the stream of consciousness.

Symbol Sets, & Reality

The language of dreams is filled with symbols which, unlike words, always resonate with many meanings on many levels. Our psychic perceptions also are filled with symbols that speak on many levels. This is necessary because in both dreaming and in psychic perception different levels of the self are in dialogue and symbols are broad enough to span the differences between the various levels and parts of the self. To more fully understand your perceptions of subtle energies you must broaden your conscious knowledge of symbols and deepen your capacity to plumb the depths of symbols.

The broadening and deepening of your conscious knowledge of symbols is a paradoxical and contradictory process. Until there is balance between these two aims there will be false starts and perhaps even losses in capacity to resolve and to understand perceptions. When a balance between the depth and the breadth of your symbol sets is maintained you will have left the awkward adolescence of rapid growth and will be ready for more a precise understanding of your psychic perceptions.

Broadening of your understanding of symbols may involve researching the pantheons and mythos of various cultures or the music of various contemporary subcultures from Country to Grunge Rock to World Beat. It may mean reading books about advertising, or heraldry, or psychology. In enlarging the range of possible symbols that you are consciously aware of you give yourself a greater vocabulary to make sense of what the parts of yourself that are non-verbal and non-linear wish to convey. The nonverbal and nonlinear parts of yourself are where psychic perceptions are processed before they are to be passed on to your conscious self. If those parts of self lack appropriate symbolic language to describe a perception, that perception may be discarded, and never reach the level of consciousness.

This greater vocabulary may also be confusing until the meanings and associations become clear. Symbols are invariably parts of sets, they exist within a resonant matrix of associations with other symbols. Symbols come in families and families are related to other families. An example of this is the parallel between Greek and Roman mythologies as represented by the sisterly relation between Aphrodite and Venus or further afield as represented by their Norse cousin Freya.

In verbal language you can sometimes derive the meaning of an unknown word by its context. The same is true for unknown symbols. If you know the tradition, culture or time period that a symbol came from something of its meaning can be deduced. Broadening your knowledge of symbol sets is like learning several languages. If you know French and Spanish it is probable that you will be able to make a good guess at the meaning of an Italian word. If you are learning French, Spanish, and Italian at the same time it is more than likely that you will confuse words from one language to another until they have been fully assimilated.

Deepening your understanding of the meanings of a symbol or of a set of symbols is a slower process than broadening your knowledge of symbols. It is difficult to do both at the same time because the modes of assimilation which broaden and the modes of assimilation which deepen are similar but distinctly different. It is like the relationship between microcosms and macrocosms as expressed in: "As above, so below, but in a different manner."

Meditation on a symbol is a time-proven way to gain deeper and more intimate understanding. In meditation on a symbol you may find assistance in your work by using your senses to support your inner work. This may be done with music, a painting or diagram to focus on, an object to hold, appropriate incense, or some other cue that keys into the symbol. Another suggestion is to seek out good dictionaries and books on etymology to delve for the roots of the words that describe the symbols that you are studying. Be patient with yourself. Knowledge can be gained relatively quickly but discernment takes time, and wisdom takes even longer. On some levels you may already have depths of understanding but it takes time to build a path from those levels to your waking consciousness. More so than broadening your knowledge, deepening your understanding is a very personal process that involves integrating new insights with the meanings that you bring from your upbringing, your culture, and your environment.

Consistency

The analysis of your perceptions of subtle energies is more like the interpretation of poetry or paintings than it is like the identification of herbs with an illustrated field guide at hand. Consistency of meaning for the colors, images, sounds, and symbols you may perceive is consistent within the context of a particular act of psychic work but may not carry over past that *particular* moment. This may seem frustrating or liberating to you depending upon your state of mind. Thankfully when working with psychic perceptions and subtle energies there is some degree of consistency because the energy patterns that you are working with ultimately have a grounding in the physical body. Magick or energy work that deals with living things have form restrictions as a result of the laws of matter and the physical plane of reality. Magick or energy work that deals with non-corporeal beings also respond to the laws and form restrictions relative to their plane of origin.

To maximize the amount and the value of the consistency of meaning in energy or magical work many symbol sets and systems of correspondences have been developed. Various magical orders, lodges, and traditions ascribe specific meanings to colors, sounds, or symbols that are consistent within their own framework, but often are not comparable between magical orders, lodges, and traditions. This incompatibility has generated many unnecessary frictions and misunderstandings between practitioners over the years. You may ask what is the truth after examining a variety of systems? The answer is a powerful and sometimes misused paradox: it is intent, coherence, and applicability that validates magical systems in a reciprocal relationship between the system and the reality that it models. An effective symbol system works to a great degree by the principle of sympathetic magic.

This does not mean that anything goes because there are restrictions both in form limitations and in linear time so long as you are operating in or around the physical plane. It does mean that there is great flexibility in what will work. The way that chakras are described in Yoga is no better than how they are described in Theosophy. As an example, if you see a wooden object with four legs and a flat area you may say *table* or if you speak Spanish you may say *mesa*. Both table and mesa are ascribed to the same physical reality and both are right. However, the two words "table" and "mesa" are only useful within the boundaries of their system which in this case is their language. Words, and for that matter magickal symbols, it should be remembered are a form of notation. In a song book, the lines of musical notes and the lines of lyrics are each necessary. The utility of the musical notes and lyrics is dependent upon their placement in the context of their own system. There is little to gain and much to lose by jumbling the notes and the words together.

In assessing the value of a symbol system it is important to be aware of which planes or levels of reality that the system is native to. Newton described the physics of motion in a set of laws that are still perfectly usable in daily life. Einstein, several centuries later, devised laws that describe space, time, and motion in situations unusual to daily life and also described motions and actions that are invisible to human senses. It is pointless to say that either Newton's way or Einstein's way is better because it is a question of which *level* not right or wrong.

The models for the behavior of subtle energies have been developed in a variety of ways. The four main ways that these systems have been developed is through the work of the conscious mind, of cultures, of archetypes, and of the unconscious. Examples of systems of symbols include Astrology, the Tarot, the Qabala, Hermetics, and folklore. Each of these systems was developed and continues to develop through these four ways that have been described in some detail by Jungian psychology. We will return to discussing this fourfold pattern later in this book.

However important a solid knowledge of symbols may be it is more important to remember that symbols are not the same thing as the reality that they describe. In opening yourself to sensing and resolving energies and patterns in a meaningful fashion you embark upon the path of an artist in search of their own style. Whether you do this as a member of a school or movement or as an iconoclast is also your choice.

Roadblocks To Clarity And Effectiveness

Of the possible sources of interference with your conscious interactions with subtle energies, three merit close examination. The first of the three is your own inner issues. Aside from the more apparent considerations such as lack of practice or of focus that can interfere with your work there are less apparent issues such as low self esteem or fear of power. You may wish to ask yourself what does it mean to you to be able to sense and work with magick? Do you trust the different parts of yourself that lie outside your waking consciousness? Are you exhausted or stressed beyond your capacity to cope? What is your intent and the level of your sincerity in this work? As with all magical or psychic development the first and central work is that of the evolution of the self.

Cultural issues can also impact on the quality and clarity of psychic perceptions. Just as your cultural background leaves its distinctive mark on your diet, health, and assumptions— it also leaves its imprint on your aura and chakras in the way of thought forms. This can cause distortions and deviations from reality directly or indirectly as an artifact of your cultural pattern or as a reaction to the cultural pattern of those people you work with. Additionally, in the United States most people come from a mixture of cultures and are heir to the positive and the negative interactions of their different heritages and archetypes.

The environment also has a part to play in how clear or effective you may be in magickal work. The environment exists in both time, space, and your interactions with it and all the other beings present. The prevailing energy *weather* is the sum of the astrological conditions, the season of the year, the time of day, and the physical weather. This energy weather in turn is added to the energy of your location which is determined by factors such as ley lines, the patterns imprinted on the place over time, the local elemental forces, and physical factors related to geology and geomagnetism. Lastly, the summation of these influences modify and are modified by your energy field and that of any others present.

Conclusion

It may becoming clear that in working with subtle energies we have numerous options, but that as it is with most magickal work we are neither bound nor free in our choices or approach. If the issues raised or the complexity of the subject matter seem daunting take heart in that you need only move at your own pace. Be prepared for delightful consequences as you open yourself to these experiences because they will spill over into other parts of your life. Be also prepared to endure the difficulties involved in learning more about yourself through this work. You find some food for thought on page 34 that you may wish to study after working through the exercises.

Exercises

Just as an athlete must warm up and limber up to do their best it is important to prepare the mind before engaging in psychic work. As a warm up to holding a complete realization in your mind the five basic senses will first need to be stretched and limbered. Even if you are quite familiar with meditation and visualization you may find benefit by following the sequence of this exercise.

Place your body in a comfortable sitting position that feels relaxed but not slouched. Close your eyes and breathe deeply and regularly to release tension and stress. If you have pressing worries or concerns identify them and tell yourself that you will come back to them at the end of the exercise but that for the time being the concerns will be set aside. If you normally use some technique for meditation or as a preparation of magickal or psychic work you may use it at this time also. When you feel reasonably comfortable and relaxed you are ready to begin.

Sight

- In your mind's eye see a white square against a field of black. Hold that image until you have clearly seen the four sides of the square, then fill the inside of the square with the color blue. Change the color of the square as many times as you like until you feel that it is becoming easier to hold both the shape and the color in mind. If you have difficulty visualizing colors have a collection of pieces of colored paper in front of you during the exercise and periodically open your eyes and peek at them to reset your sense of color.

If you are skilled at visualization you may add these additional steps to this part of the exercise. Turn the square into a cube in your mind's eye. When the cube is solid slowly begin to rotate it. After doing this exercise several times you may wish to visualize a circle/sphere, a triangle/pyramid, an ellipse/egg, or other simple geometric forms.

Sound

- Say your own name out loud, clap your hands, and tap a glass with a spoon or fork. Wait for a moment then replay those sounds in your mind. Wait again for a moment then replay the sounds in reverse sequence: clinking glass, hand clap, your voice. Then take five slips of paper, think of five familiar sounds and write down a sound on each slip. As an example the sounds might be: dog bark, car horn, running faucet, door slam, guitar chord. Take the slips place them in a glass and draw them out one by one. As you draw them out pause to hear each sound in your mind. Return the slips to the glass and repeat this exercise several times. The sounds should be different each time that you do this exercise.

Touch

Run your index finger across the palm of your hand while carefully noting the sensation in both your finger tip and on your palm. Repeat this several times and then call up those same sensations in your mind. When you can reproduce those sensations in your mind you are ready for the next part of the exercise. Imagine your finger touching the top of your left big toe. Slowly move this imaginary finger across the top of your foot, up your shin, your thigh, up your hips, stomach, chest, neck, up the left side of your face and then stop at the crown of your head. After pausing at the crown of your head continue with your imaginary finger down the right side of the back of your head, down your right shoulder blade, lower back, buttocks, back of the right thigh, back of the knee, the leg, the Achilles tendon, and the sole of the the right foot, and come around and finish on the top of the big right toe. At first this may not be easy to do in one continuous effort so you may need to break it up into manageable chunks.

Smell

Go to your kitchen and select four spices or foods that have distinct odors. An example of this would be vanilla extract, onions, canned pet food, and mustard. Smell each of the four items, allowing time in between for your nose to clear, then set them aside. Call up each of the odors in your mind one by one until you have successfully captured each scent. Pick one of the four odors that you selected and hold it under your nose once more. While sniffing at it with your physical nose call up the three other scents one by one in your mind. The goal of this part of the exercise is to be able to hold the imagined scent in mind at the same time that a strong familiar odor is present. When you repeat this exercise you may alternate which odor is the one that is under your nose as well as the selection of the four odors.

Taste

In front of yourself place a glass of water and small amounts of the following: salt, sugar (or honey or a sugar substitute), vinegar or lemon juice, and epsom salts or baking soda. Taste a small amount of each of the four making sure to sip water to clear your palate between each substance. Focus your attention sharply on the categories of flavor called salty, sweet, sour, and bitter as you taste these four substances. Now take another sip of water and imagine that the water tastes sweet and sour. Test the accuracy of your mind's tongue by placing a pinch of sugar and a drop of vinegar on your tongue. You may also try other combinations and experiment with spices. Please be gentle to your digestive system in your experiments with your sense of taste. Use the smallest amounts necessary and always finish with a glass of water.

Realization

Select a type of raw fruit or vegetable that you like to eat, perhaps apples, carrots, celery, or grapes. Read through this exercise at least once before using it and create a set of cues and questions that are appropriate to the fruit or vegetable that you select. For the purposes of description I will use an apple in my example. Close your eyes and realize yourself sitting at a table. Place your arms on the table and feel the solid support of the table. How does your body feel? What does the chair you are in sitting feel like? On the table there is a white porcelain bowl filled with different types of apples. See the patterns of light and dark and color made by the mound of apples. You reach over and pick one up. How does it feel? How heavy does it feel? Is the apple firm or does it have mushy spots? Sniff it and look closely at the grain and the color of the skin. You take a bite feel it give against the pressure of your teeth. Is it dry or juicy. Is it sweet and/or tart? Is it crisp or mealy? As you chew feel the sensations in your jaws and mouth. Is there juice on your lips or chin? When you swallow follow it down your esophagus and feel the fullness slowly grow in your belly. Continue until you have eaten everything but the core. Look a the core. Are there seeds visible? Do your fingers or face feel sticky?

Immediately after finishing the exercise look around the room and compare your sensory experience of the room with the experience of the exercise. If you have the energy to do so, repeat the exercise immediately after making the comparison. If you cannot do this, make notes that you can read before attempting the exercise again.

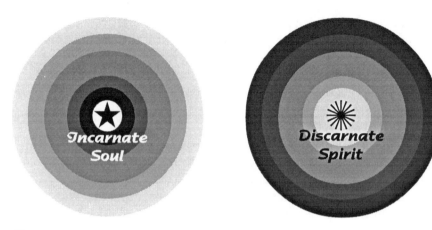

In sensing and making sense of energy and information you may consider the part of you that is here on the physical plane as one end of a continuum with the part of you that is eternal and outside of linear time as the other end. All Information/Energy must pass through each level before it can progress to the next and blockages or misalignments at any level can modify, modulate, or stop the flow.

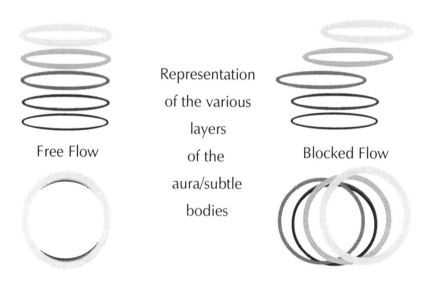

5

Grounding & Centering

This chapter's objective is to provide concise explanations for those that are new to grounding and centering and to refresh the perspectives of old hands in the use of energy and consciousness. Before proceeding with using any of the castings I would recommend that you take time to reflect on the importance of grounding and centering. The format of this chapter is a series of commonly asked questions about grounding and centering followed by short responses. Regardless of your level of experience in magickal matters, I believe that you will find useful ideas and methods worthy of testing in the following paragraphs. After the questions and answers there is an exercise that encourages an experience of grounding and centering.

Familiarity may or may not breed contempt, but it certainly can drain away magic through the gutter of complacency. The words *grounding* and *centering* are part of the idiom widely used by modern seekers of old mysteries. In the rush for results, that often plagues contemporary society, grounding and centering often cease to be idioms or terms of art, and become jargon or buzz words. Grounding and centering are as basic and as important to working with sacred space as arithmetic is to algebra. Buzz words, like pocket calculators, may speed results, but the accuracy and utility of the results are only as good as the knowledge and the understanding of the user.

"What Is Grounding?"

Anodea Judith writes in *Wheels Of Life* that, "Grounding is a process of dynamic contact with the Earth, with its edges, boundaries, and limitations. Through a combination of relaxation and energizing we allow our subtle energy to condense and solidify." [1] Grounding is connecting with our bodies to affirm their importance before shifting our focus outwards to encompass more than the physical, and more than ourselves. Grounding is also an affirmation of the interconnectedness of all living things on Earth. We live in a culture that mistrusts, misuses, and misunderstands the physical. Within that context, those that are seeking health and wholeness need to remember the

---

[1]   Anodea Judith, *Wheels of Life* (Llewellyn) p. 68. This is an excellent book on chakras.

value and the wisdom of their bodies, and of all life. It is through the instrument of our bodies that we experience our lives, and interact with others.

As with all things physical, the body has limits, and a range of conditions within which the body can function with health and efficiency. If these parameters are exceeded, temporary or permanent damage may result. The same is true for our subtle (nonphysical energy) bodies, although their parameters are different. Grounding doesn't expand these parameters, but it does bring into play the safety net of the Earth's capacity to absorb energy that is excess or of an improper frequency. Psychologically and spiritually, grounding is also an admission that you do have limits, and are open to receive assistance. Grounding clarifies limits and boundaries at the same time that it shows the interconnectedness and unity of all things. Grounding closes the circuit of the *inner*, and the *outer* in order to allow energy to flow freely, and safely.

Since moving into sacred or magickal space through castings is a movement into a reality filled with a broader range of energies the need for grounding is paramount. As more layers of subtle bodies or different parts of self become engaged the potential for overload increases. Most of us are unaccustomed to the strain of exerting more of our *selves*, and like the weekend athlete may stumble into injuries. Further, the view that castings in part function through the power of the microcosm/macrocosm axiom and/or the holographic paradigm indicates that the effort at clarifying boundaries and interconnectedness that is an integral part of grounding increases the effectiveness of castings. Psychologically and spiritually the process of grounding also prepares us to receive help or guidance within the casting by acknowledging our limits and openness to assistance. However you frame your source(s) of help or guidance whether that be Higher Selves, Guides, Patrons, Deities, etc., it is very welcome when it is received.

"What Is Centering?"

Centering is finding balance, and true identity within yourself while being open to the flow of energy. Centering involves bringing different parts of the psyche into focus and conjunction with each other. When you are centered you are more likely to make better choices for yourself, and with others, because you will be cooperating with the various parts of yourself rather than contending against them. When your sense of your will, and intent is clear, your actions will be truer to your karma, and your life goals. The part of you that thinks with words, that is reading this article, is an equal partner with those parts of you that think in images, dreams, and music. Centering establishes a meeting place for your Child Self, your Higher Self, your Shadow, and all the Selves that comprise your whole. Centering means seeking the core of true authenticity, and security that nurtures us. Mary Caroline Richards, a poet and a potter, writes, "Centering: that act which precedes all others on the potter's wheel. The bringing of the clay into a spinning, unwobbling pivot, which will then be free to take innumerable shapes as potter and clay press against each other." [2] When we are centered we are most able to shape and to be shaped by our lives.

The stability of a casting, like the stability of the clay on the wheel, is to a great degree dependent upon your own still, center, point. The whirl of subtle energies called forth by a casting is not able to hold a coherent pattern for very long without your stillness. Aside from concerns related to the stability and the efficacy of a casting, the question of clarity of intent and the karma resulting from magickal actions is directly related to centering. Although there are many ways to conceptualize how karma works, one common thread is the belief that *intent* sets the tone for the causal manifestations of karma. In most cases, each of us has a variety of intents and levels of ambivalence arising from our many sub-personalities and parts of self. Be very careful of what you wish for— especially when it's wishing by committee. The act of centering helps to bring some focus, or at least balance, to our intent which in turn impacts upon our choices, and the resulting consequences. It helps to generate a consensus in the self rather than the rule of the loudest voice.

"How Will I Know I'm Grounded And Centered?"

As individuals we perceive grounding and centering in a way that makes sense relative to the other ways we use physical sensations as adjuncts, or as metaphors for states of being. An example of this type of perception by metaphor would be that some people identify when their jaw is tight they are resisting something, and when their throat is tight they have something to say but haven't been able to give it voice. In grounding and centering there are usually bodily sensations that can be discovered as your individual signposts towards reaching the desired state. For myself, grounding most often feels like my body has become larger, sometimes vast, but still agile; centering feels like my consciousness has come to rest on a soft pillow, supported but unencumbered. In addition to your senses of balance and body awareness, consider your five basic senses in mapping out the set of sensations that correspond to grounding and centering for you.

Grounding and centering are a balance achieved through dynamic processes not static conditions. This means that they exist in linear time, and must be maintained. In fact, the closer one gets to being fully grounded and cen-

---

[2] Mary Caroline Richards, *Centering: In Pottery, Poetry, and the Person* (Wesleyan University Press, Connecticut, 1972) p. 9

tered the harder it is to maintain that state. In grounding, as you connect with more, and more of the Earth's life, and energy ecology, you must accommodate an exponentially larger network. In centering, as more parts of your psyche come into play, you eventually begin to move from the personal to the transpersonal, and to identities that like dreams fade quickly when held in the grasp of waking consciousness. Part of the nature of being physical is that there are no absolutes, but this does not mean that we cannot strive for ideals.

While in sacred space, you may need to ground and center numerous times over the course of a ritual or working. At first this may feel cumbersome, but it soon becomes no more difficult than clapping and singing at the same time. Indeed, over the course of time this can become an important part of the transition into your magickal persona or headspace. If the feel of being grounded and centered becomes associated with your sense of being in your magickal identity you will have greater ease in most of your castings.

"I Like That Really Charged Up Feeling. Won't Grounding Take That Away Or Make Me Feel Drained?"

Yes and no. You will release any energy that you do not need and/or is not yours to keep at that time. If you feel tired after grounding ask yourself whether it feels like the pleasant fatigue that follows hard work, or is it the run down feeling you associate with a cold or flu? If you still feel charged up after grounding does it feel like the alertness that follows a healthy breakfast after a good night's sleep, or does it remind you of the jittery sharpness of too many cups of caffeine? You can glean useful information from assessing your sensations after grounding. Feeling run down may indicate that you were drawing too heavily upon your own energy, or were not open to energy from outside yourself. Feeling jittery may mean that you are hanging on to a scrap of excess energy in order to validate the experience, or perhaps to seek sensation for its own sake. Your sensations may not mean any of these things, but they will mean something.

It is understandable to want some form of tangible validation as feedback on the progress or actuality of a casting, but I suggest that opening to your psychic senses and perceptions is a more profitable route. Not only will your psychic perceptions provide you with more detailed feedback so that you can refine your castings, but they will help to alleviate the desire to over-experience. Additionally, the more you practice psychic perception the stronger and sharper it will become which may benefit other endeavors.

"What Happens If I Don't Ground And Center?"

Perhaps nothing — perhaps something unpleasant. If energy is raised or altered, and is not put to a use, such as healing, meditation, visioning, or it is not entirely released the undirected energy can result in symptoms of disease. After practical applications of spiritual or metaphysical workings if you feel spacey, light-headed, have a headache, or experience some other discomfort, physical or mental, it may well be that you weren't sufficiently grounded. If too much of the energy was diverted because of improper grounding there may be no results worthy of noting. If after a healing, an affirmation, or some other action the results are unwanted and/or unexpected, there may have been a lack of centering to focus intent. Our bodies, hearts, and higher selves do look out for us. To some degree we always ground and center, whether or not the effort is a conscious one, but when we cooperate consciously the outcome is fuller.

Re-entry into normal reality can be harsh, depending on the casting or the work done between the worlds. If you don't ground and center you give up an opportunity to soften and to speed the transition. Speaking pragmatically, this is essential since it is rare in our hectic times to have the luxury of ample time after a ritual or working before returning to mundane schedules and activities.

"When Should I Ground & Center?"

Ground and center before, during, and after any work that raises energy or alters energy. The entry into sacred space is considered an alteration of energy. This simple guideline is difficult to follow. If the question is *when* is it most critical to ground and center, the answer would be at the end of a working in order to minimize or to eliminate the effects of any unused or unbalanced energy. Grounding and centering is also useful during stressful episodes in our lives to help to manage stress. In an ideal world we would be grounded and centered almost every moment of our lives.

There are certain rituals or workings that do call for very brief periods during which you exceed your normal energy capacity for specific purposes, but they are the exception— not the rule. Use your judgment, and listen for guidance, as to whether these momentary surges are reasonable and acceptable. There are also techniques to make contact with or to assume aspects of God/ dess/es and other entities that involve a modification of the center point to accommodate higher forces and presences. To reach this synthetic balance a span of uncentered instability is often traversed. Again, heed your own inner voice in these matters.

"Why Isn't Grounding And Centering
Part Of Every Tradition?"

Upon close examination, you will find, though the language, and the metaphors may change from tradition to tradition, and from culture to culture, the basis for grounding and centering is usually present. Cultures can and do vary dramatically; hence the methods that individuals, as members of cultures, use in spiritual practices range as widely as the differences between individuals, and between cultures. In some cases it is difficult to recognize the manner in which grounding and centering is accomplished. In Native American traditions it is the culture itself, the beliefs and folkways, that grounds those that are connected to the culture. The cultures of Western people tend to alienate them from, rather than to connect them to nature; therefore a separate, regular, conscious effort to ground and center is important, if not necessary.

Castings are highly culture dependent and belief system dependent so the form that grounding and centering takes relative to the casting is highly variable. Give free rein to your creativity in weaving grounding and centering into the pattern of your ritual work. Unless you are truly immersed and confirmed in a culture that is Earth-centered, I would think it crucial that grounding and centering not be left to chance or catch as catch can.

"More Questions?"

Hopefully one of the outcomes of reading this chapter is that you will ask more detailed questions on working with consciousness and energy in the circles, events, and the workshops that you attend. More questions, and some answers, will also be the outcome of seeking to better experience grounding and centering. If you choose to try the visualization exercise that follows, please feel free to fine tune the imagery to your own sensibilities. You may wish to make a tape of the exercise to facilitate its use.

Grounding & Centering Exercise

Place your body in a comfortable position and close your eyes. Breathe deeply and slowly. If you have any pressing concerns or worries set them aside. Tell your troubles that you will return to them later but that for now you wish to lay your burdens down. Listen to the sounds of your surroundings, and when you are certain that all is well, tune those sounds out of your conscious awareness. Let tension seep away from your body. Let each deep slow breath carry away all discomfort and fill you with wellbeing.

Grounding & Centering

Imagine a forest in late Spring. Imagine that you are becoming a tree in the midst of this forest. Your feet are sprouting roots that are delving down into the ground. Roots that are strong and thick as well as delicate and gentle. Your roots are slipping through the soil, embracing the ever larger stones that they find as they dig deeper. Your roots taste the soil. Feel the cool moistness. Your roots intertwine with the roots of the other plants and trees that surround you. Your roots and the roots of all the trees that you sense around you are digging downwards towards the Earth's core. The Earth's core is a fiery sphere of molten rock and your roots reach towards it. Feel the warmth. Reach for the fiery sphere. Feel the pulse of energy rising from your roots into your trunk.

Now imagine that your arms and hands are boughs and branches reaching upwards to the sky. Feel the breezes move through the leaves that are your fingers. Smell the breezes. As you reach upwards towards the blazing ball of the sun, feel the light touches of the leaves and the branches of other trees reaching skywards with you. Feel the warmth of the sun upon your leaves, your branches, and your boughs. Feel the energy enter your leaves and join the pulse of energy that is your life sap.

Sense the sun above you and the fire of the Earth's core below. Feel the pulse of your circulating life fluids. All the fullness of energy to permeate your every cell.

Become aware of the center of your consciousness, the point that is the seat of your awareness. Let your center of consciousness float freely, up and down in your trunk. Take some time letting it move as it will. Let your consciousness float until it finds a place of stillness and balance between the sun above and the fire below.

Affirm that you are grounded and you are centered.

Suggestions

• If there is a type of tree that holds fond associations for you choose that variety. If you can't think of one then look out the window or in a book or magazine to freshen the details in your mind's eye of what a tree looks like.

• As an addition to the visualization, at the end of a working touching the ground with your hands and/or forehead is an effective way to ground quickly, and more thoroughly.

• If you have difficulty in locating your center point, it may be helpful to you to find your physical balance point. Stand up and feel the weight distribution through your body. Lift one leg and balance on one foot and then close your eyes. Try to find where you feel balanced and make a note of where the center of your consciousness seems to be when your body is balanced. If you are unable to stand or easily lose your balance, you may gain a similar benefit by swaying with your eyes closed in a seated position and noting the place that your awareness hinges upon in the motion.

• If the tree exercise doesn't work for you create a visualization for yourself using the seed image of a outcropping of rock by the ocean as a starting point. The following passage may give you further food for thought:

> "Sea and Stone Are Deep In Life.
> Permanence in Motion, And Permanence At Rest." [3]

---

[3] Stephen Donaldson, *The Chronicles Of Thomas Covenant The Unbeliever,* Nelson Doubleday Inc., 1977

6

Immanence, Transcendence, & Magickal Reality

This chapter is primarily theoretical with few immediate and apparent applications to castings or practical magick, so you may be tempted to skip forwards. If you do so, I suspect that you'll find your way back to this short discussion of a few aspects of magickal reality. Not unlike the relationship between science and technology, metaphysics, mythology, and philosophy are the root sources of castings, magick, and practical workings. Conversely, our experience or our refinement of techniques lead to new awarenesses of the theoretical. The abstract and the concrete are always engaged in interchange and exchange.

Our appreciation of journeys into sacred space are colored by the vehicles that we use as our mode of transport. A journey by train, bicycle, or hot air balloon would all lead to very different impressions even if the route and the destination were the same. Different castings, of themselves, will help to set the routes, and the destinations of journeys into other realities, but they are not vehicles per se. You are both the vehicle, the driver, and the passenger. What shape that vehicle takes depends upon your sense of the nature of what is sacred, and hence the structure of reality.

In the 17th century Baruch Spinoza taught that reality is a unity, of one substance, with an infinity of possible and actual attributes of which the human mind can grasp but a few—chiefly thought and its extensions. In a related way, your experience of sacred space is limited to a few attributes, the number and type of which are set by your viewpoint, and the clarity of your vision. Corroboration for this assertion can be found in the similarities and the differences found in examining the stories of people who have had a metaphysical encounter. As an example: people who have had near death experiences with similar cultural or religious backgrounds generally see and report compatible symbols and events. Comparing near death experiences cross-culturally leads to less congruent results. Christians see the door to light through Christ, or Mary, or perhaps Peter and his Pearly Gates. Wiccans may see the door to Summerland or Arianrhod's Spiral Castle. Indeed the similari-

43

ties that do exist in cross-cultural comparisons may still be cultural bias rather than an indication of an over-arching truth because of the shared history of many traditions.

Over the last several thousand years the paradigm of transcendence has nearly reached supremacy as the world's touchstone for the divine. Currently, the paradigm of immanence is beginning to reintroduce itself into the common culture. In the uncertainty of our times there is a tendency to create exclusionary dichotomies, so many feel the need to choose one paradigm over the other. This choice is at least unnecessary if not actually harmful. I believe that your personal definition, understanding, and model for the concepts of immanence and transcendence establish the basis for your perspective and your viewpoint on the nature of the sacred. Robert Scholes wrote, "For truth is like ordinary light, present everywhere but invisible, and we must break it to behold it."[1] Through the prism of our concepts of immanence, transcendence, and reality we divide that part of the broad spectrum of truth that we can sense into the colors of visible light.

Immanence

In religions, systems of mystical thought, and cosmologies that hold immanence as their primary perspective, divinity is seen as all pervasive within manifest reality. In its purest form, immanence shows divinity as arising from the sum of nature that is greater than all its parts. The concept of immanence in its most extreme form indicates that divinity may not violate the laws of nature. A consequence of this seed idea is polytheistic, multitheistic, and animistic religions. There are gradations rather than divisions between spirit and matter in this perspective. This belief affirms the value of the physical as a means to grow in spirit. Immanence implies that much of what constitutes deity is accessible through the senses (both physical and psychic). There is a tendency to view time as moving in cycles with many possible futures. Life is seen as a worthy experience in and of itself. The continued existence of an individual's essence after death is *not* required by this perspective. A system based on immanence is predisposed to hold as tenets: evolution, an openended universe, and the free will of beings as capable of resulting in outcomes that are not planned by divinity.

Transcendence

In religions, systems of mystical thought, and cosmologies that hold Transcendence as their primary perspective, divinity is seen existing outside of the physical universe. In its purest form, transcendence shows divinity as

---

[2]   Robert Scholes, *Elements of Fiction* (Oxford University Press, New York, 1968) p.4

creating and governing all of nature. The concept of transcendence in its most radical form indicates that divinity may violate all the laws of nature. A consequence of this seed idea is monotheistic, hierarchical religions. There is a clear division between spirit and matter in this perspective. This division often leads to a stance that states that spirit is superior to matter, or in its most extreme case— that matter is evil. Transcendence implies that much of what constitutes deity is not accessible through the senses (both physical and psychic). There is a tendency to view time as a linear construct with an orderly, predestined future. Life is seen as a preparatory experience for the afterlife. The continued existence of an individual's essence after death is *required* by this perspective. A system based on transcendence is predisposed to hold as tenets: progress, a bounded universe, and the free will of beings as ultimately acting within a greater plan.

Immanence and Transcendence as Polarity

If regarded as a dichotomy these two paradigms create opposing and irreconcilable world-views. If immanence and transcendence are regarded as a polarity their union and reconciliation become inevitable. Polarity, in the metaphysical sense, reveals an underlying unity between the things held as opposites just as the North pole and the South pole of a magnet are unified by the common force of magnetism. Polarity also infers that one could not exist without the other and/or that the existence of one calls forth the existence of the other. Helena Blavatsky, the founder of the modern Theosophical movement, taught that without polarity manifestation was impossible. When a polarity is misunderstood, or poorly utilized, there is tension and erratic shifts in the balance between the two opposing forces. When the polarity is understood there is greater awareness of the meaning of each pole, and of all the gradations that span the extremes. Well utilized, polarity is a powerful source of energy.

No Pure Forms

Paradigms, no matter how highly refined they may be, are forms and as such are subject to the limits of forms. One of those limits is that no form can be pure while in the realm of matter. True purity, like Platonic *ideals*, can only exist in planes far distant from the ones we inhabit. In terms of this discussion this means that any model for representing divinity (sacred force and pattern) within the universe must be an admixture of the forms of immanence and of transcendence. In other words, all religions or systems of spiritual thought use both immanence and transcendence as ingredients in their formulation regardless of what their doctrine may state.

Magickal Reality

In a very demonstrable way reality is always a personal and a subjective approximation of whatever the objective truth may be. Two individuals may look at the same painting and share their impressions with each other. They may even use the same or similar words to describe the colors and the shapes, but what they see is personal and different. Visual acuity and color perception varies dramatically. Sensibilities and past experiences alter the meanings of the words used to describe the painting by attaching connotations that may be unique to each individual. In a limited fashion, we do indeed create our own reality every moment of our lives.

In daily life it is important that the reality we create for ourselves be communicable and intelligible to other people. This is one of the benchmarks frequently used to ascertain sanity. Unlike the daily reality that we share with others, much like performers sharing and reinterpreting folk songs that have developed and changed over time, a personal magickal reality is a construct composed by an individual with intent. Magickal reality is a quirky, individual experience that is usually only partly communicable to others. The fluidity of magickal reality is one of its strengths and weaknesses. Its nature is less cohesive than the reality of daily life, so it becomes crucial to instill pattern and coherence in its creation.

Your personal understanding of immanence and transcendence are important keys in the composition of a personal magickal reality. In sifting through the various systems, traditions, and religions you may find these prevalent magickal beliefs:

Planes

The universe consists of a number of planes or dimensions that vary in density of material, vibration or frequency, rate and type of time, and other factors. Depending upon the system, these planes may exist adjacent to each other, interpenetrate, line up like rungs in a ladder, or relate to each other in a multitude of ways. There is often confusion or dissension related to the planes because different systems claim different numbers of planes with clashing attributions. It is my belief that the truth of the planes is much more like the continuum of the spectrum of light. For practical purposes we break up the spectrum into colors that we can name, but we may not agree on where to draw the line between blue and green. Similarly, there many distinct musical scales that break up the spectrum of sound for different musical intentions. Nonetheless, there are commonalities between the systems. Many Eastern and Western systems attribute high density and low frequency vibrations to the plane of matter and lessening density and higher frequency vibrations as we rise on the planes towards absolute spirit.

Subtle Bodies

A natural outcome of the system of planes is the belief that we have many bodies— not just our physical forms. Our subtle bodies, subtle meaning: composed of less dense matter/energy vibrating at frequencies not normal to the physical, also correspond to their own states of consciousness (see appendix on Chakras). When we are grounded and centered our subtle bodies are brought into greater alignment. The alignment of our subtle bodies is highly desirable because it facilitates the flow of information and energy between the bodies. We may perceive psychic impressions through the anchoring medium of our physical senses, but the actual organs of psychic perception are in the subtle bodies. Moreover, when we engage in ritual, our actions on the physical plane have their correlate action in our subtle bodies. Much of the actual *work* in ritual is done by our subtle bodies.

The Journey of Spirit Into Matter

Repeated in most spiritual systems is the motif of spirit entering into the realm of matter then returning to the plane of spirit. Building upon the core tenets of a system of belief, this motif may be a linear process based on one lifetime or a cycle of reincarnations. There are many possible permutations for the journey of spirit into matter, and as many meanings. The purpose of this cycle is often the education of the individual for the enrichment of the whole. In most systems, complete union with the Source marks the end of the cycle of incarnation.

One of the stories used in my Tradition to describe this cycle compares the individual to a daffodil. From the darkness of the soil, the womb of earth, a new life springs forth and reaches upwards towards the light. In the fullness of its growth it blooms and the flower reflects the light of the Sun and the Moon, the Divine. The flower represents the Soul and the unique summation of the interaction between Matter and Spirit within an individual incarnation. After a time the flower fades, the work is done. The life force leaves the visible plane of the Earth to enrich the bulb which represents the Spirit that is growing and evolving through seasons of lives. In the Spring a new incarnation brings a new flower, a new Soul, but it is an expression of the Spirit that persists from cycle to cycle.

Time and Eternity

Time is seen as having many possible manifestations. It can exist in a linear fashion moving from past to future with the present as a continually shifting point like a swiftly flowing river. It can exist as possibilities branching, meandering, joining and separating like a river delta. It can be a plane, like the ocean stretching in every direction. Like light, time is both a particle and a wave. Eternity exists outside of Time and encompasses it, as Spirit encompasses Soul. If Time is a line then Eternity is the paper. The relationship between Eternity and Time is the key to understanding the unfolding of the individuated expression we call a Soul within a lifetime against the backdrop of the Spirit that spans all the lives.

In my Tradition we believe that Time and Eternity relate to the planes of reality as a continuum of proportions. On the physical plane linear Time is predominant and Eternity is weak. As we rise on the planes Eternity strengthens and linear Time weakens (see figure below). One of the outcomes inherent in these relationships is a spectrum of relative influence between the forces of causality and the forces of synchronicity.

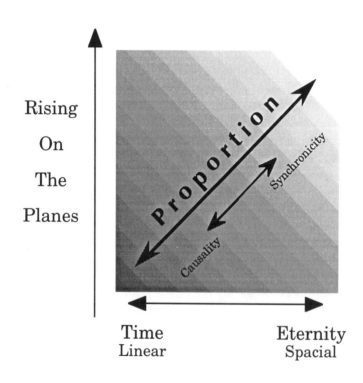

7

The Quarters: Space, Time, & Elements

Calling the Quarters, which is to say invoking the powers of the four directions, is an integral part of most Western systems for the creation of sacred space. The Quarters, which in this book will refer to any four-fold categorization or division of the mythic whole, could be studied for a lifetime, and that would only be a preliminary study. The goal of this chapter is more modest; it will provide you with the starting points and benchmarks. Each of the explorations of these special attributes or correspondences for the Quarters contain useful references for all the castings not just those that call them directly.

Alignments In Space, Time, And The Body

As I indicated earlier, before beginning any journey into sacred space you must first get your bearings. In their seed state, the Quarters are about living on the surface of planet Earth and recognizing our relationship to space and to time. Let's see how that seed idea sprouts and unfolds into the beginnings of magickal space. Imagine a person standing outdoors, on level ground, on the first day of spring in North America. As a result of the form and the function of the person's body and the placement of their senses, certain axes for orientation arise naturally. The person has a front, a back, and two sides, with the organs for the senses of sight and hearing placed perpendicular to each other. The special importance of the eyes and of the mouth tends to make the front the most salient direction. To stand requires attention to the pull of gravity, the body's center of balance, and the axis from the head to the feet. The nature of the human physical form supports and sponsors the validity of four directions as horizontal axes plus a vertical axis and a center. This can be seen as six directions plus center which yields the sacred number seven.

There may be a hard-wired neurological predisposition in humans towards the use of axes at 90° to each other as the default for the recognition of forms or motion. It appears, though only more research will tell, that we have sets of neurons in our brains that respond strongly and specifically to one axis and 90° degree differences. Shapes or motions that are not rectilinear are perceived by the averaging or the plotting of the deviations from these internal Cartesian coordinates. Research in cognitive psychology on the span of apprehension has also produced intriguing results. It seems that six or perhaps seven are the maximum number of channels that can be accommodated simultaneously by normal consciousness. In addition to the interesting possibilities it brings to mind in regards to axes in magickal space, it also resonates to the ordering in chakras. Science will probably continue to yield support for the wisdom of old. It should also be of no surprise that the external choices we make in how we define sacred space echo internal truths that reach down into the physical structures of our bodies, the vehicles of incarnation.

Returning to our person standing outside, imagine now that it is dawn. At the spring equinox (and the fall equinox) the sun rises in the East and sets in the West. Assuming the person has patience and fortitude, they would over the course of the day observe the Sun's path with its highest point in the South at noon[1], and its setting in the West. The Sun is directly overhead at noon only at the equator, in the Northern hemisphere its highest elevation is in the South, and in the Southern hemisphere high noon is in the North. If this incredibly patient person holds vigil through the night they will see the stars travel from East to West, and will notice a star in the North that holds steady, surrounded by an entourage of stars that rotate about it. With very little effort the natural axes that stem from the body can be correlated to the natural movements of the heavens, and the basic view of the quarters as the four cardinal directions is established. Further refinements and additional meanings arise as the Sun's path over the full cycle of a year are studied. The path of the Moon and its phases reveal many other subtle connections between inner and outer realms that will be explored in other chapters.

Since, the motions of the celestial bodies, the climate, and the ecology vary with your location on Earth, the correlations and myths that relate to the

---

[1] Real noon, the midpoint between sunrise and sunset— not the arbitrary noon set by standardized time zones. At the Solar noon the Sun is exactly in the South and is at its highest point in the sky for that day.

Quarters will be myriad. Each of these sets of correlations and correspondences, so long as they are coherent and are metaphysically sound, hold true in the mythic sense of the word, and are appropriate dependent upon individual temperaments and sensibilities. Before proceeding with a description of how to actually cast a circle I will present some of the basic correlations I use within the tradition I follow. If you find that these correlations don't work for you, look for alternate correlations that are available from a wide range of sources.

Basic Elemental Correlations

The model of the Elements also helps to unify and to redefine the polarity of matter and energy. The four phases of matter as described in physics correlate readily to the Elements. The four phases: solid, liquid, gaseous, and plasma are the counterparts of Earth, Water, Air, and Fire. Energy can probably be correlated to Ether, the fifth Element of Spirit though the correlation of space or information is equally applicable. A common mistake in efforts to gain an understanding of the Elements is to think in literal terms. Indeed many narrow minded critics of metaphysics, locked in the trap of materialism, find it incredible that in this day and age anyone could believe that all things in manifest [2] creation are composed of four elements— especially elements that are not part of the periodic table. When we speak of Air, Fire, Water, and Earth we do not mean a breeze, a flame, a drop of water, and a pebble; they are symbols expressing something of the underlying nature of physical reality. Symbols, it should be remembered, are never fully definable, but rather describe possibilities, areas of inter-relation, and *identities* with all the manifold variations that the indefinite implies.

Air is the formless, seamless, transparent, paradox from which thought and intellect arises. It is the blue sky, seemingly bound but infinite, through which the influences of the celestial bodies descend to us.It is all things that relate to cognition and the senses therefore it also is the element of psychic senses and divination. Above all else, Air is a carrier, a medium, a messenger, a facilitator, an intermediary rather than: the effect, the message, or the end in itself. We do not see the wind; we see and hear the rustle of the leaves. Air is the catalyst and the midwife for experiences. At times it appears to be a cause or an impetus because of its ability to convert the potential to the kinetic or to translate the inertia of stillness to the inertia of motion, but Air itself is moved by other forces which it transfers to all that it touches. As a result of the principle of polarity that calls forth the echo of the opposite, Air

---

[2]   Manifest is used in this sense to describe the perceivable universe both physical and subtle.

the formless, necessitates and/or creates boundaries— which are not forms, but the markers by which we identify forms. Air is the conveyer of language in the broadest sense of the word. Of the five Holy Parts of Self, Air is the Mind.

Fire is will, desire, and impetus to be and to do. It is raw vitality, sexuality, and also pure moral force and grace. Fire can be of many colors within the same flame. It is active passion as opposed to reactive emotion. It is the force that drives the purposes of incarnation. Fire is the awareness of sensations within the moment. It is the essence of purpose. While Water may ask "Why?", Fire says, "Because!". It is applied energy, kinetic— not potential. In magick, Fire is the force of directed consciousness expressed as will. Fire leaps from its fuel, grounded in matter, towards the unseen, wrapped in its own light. Fire is also spirit acting on matter from within matter. It can warm, protect, purify, or reduce to ashes. From a small spark a blaze may grow, so Fire represents the energy of fertility, fertility as physical reproduction, as creativity, as expansion, etc. Fire exists only in action; stillness destroys it. As a result of the principle of polarity that calls forth the echo of the opposite, Fire, the active element generates peace. Of the five Holy Parts of Self, Fire is the Soul.

Water is emotion in all its expressions and magnitudes, from still garden pond to crashing surf upon the rocks. It can be shallow or deep, and as easy to brush off as a stray drop of rain or as engulfing as the wide Pacific. Water attempts to process, to digest, and to transform whatever it touches, yet it takes the shape of any container, and seeks its lowest reaches. Water responds, reacts, and is acted upon. Water is magnetic in that it seeks itself, and clings to itself. Water is the synthesis of meaning from dissolved essences. It is also the Universal solvent that gives itself for life to exist. It is intuition as feeling that springs from the subconscious, unlike the intellectualized sensory psychism of Air. As a result of the principle of polarity that calls forth the echo of the opposite, Water, the processor generates action. Of the five Holy Parts of Self, Water is the Heart.

Earth is structure, the unfolding of patterns, growth, and stability. Earth is all aspects of manifestation both linear and non-linear. It is wisdom that comes from the culmination or the union of many visions and experiences. The intuition of Earth is that of instinct and of deep knowing that comes from exigency unswayed by desire. The psychism of Earth comes unbidden because it is the natural outcome and summation of what has gone before.

Earth is also material gain, wealth, health, and illness. Our bodies, all life, and the planet are formed by Earth. It is the ultimate and most powerful element on this plane of being. Of the Four Elements, Earth's sacrifice is the greatest. It is order generated by attraction, contraction, and crystallization. As a result of the principle of polarity that calls forth the echo of the opposite, Earth, the solidifier generates change. Of the five Holy Parts of Self, Earth is the Body.

Ether is the unifier that merges immanence and transcendence while retaining distinct identity. To quote one of Ferron's songs that speaks to this paradox, "It's a woman's dream this autonomy/ Where the lines connect/ And the points stay free..."[1]. Ether also reconciles paradoxes and polarities in that it is the joining of all the elements in the mystery of *becoming more than the sum of the parts*. It is also the pure and complete expression of the essence of each of the parts that make up the whole. It is as a result of the principle of polarity that calls forth the echo of the opposite, Ether, that is not any one thing, exists in every thing. Of the five Holy Parts of Self, Ether is the Spirit.

Alignments In Culture

I believe the Quarters arise from a primal substrate as deep or deeper than that of the archetypical forms that manifest in accordance with the temperament and the values of their cultures of origin. As with all deep and implicate patterns, in reality there are many ways to approach the knowing of that which lies beyond discrete definition. In the past, individuals generally learned only one suite of symbols and myths for the Quarters. This focused exposure and lifelong immersion in a *particular* way of knowing the Quarters, gave them an incredible solidity of belief and hence utility that is hard to match today. Most of the people reading this book can have access to information about literally hundreds of cultures if they so desire through other books, compact discs, videos, cd-rom discs, etc. Compared to the standards of a decade, a century, or a millennium ago, people in industrialized nations are information rich — and knowledge poor. Money can't buy happiness nor can a wealth of information buy knowledge.

It is our challenge, in this era, to learn the language of deep truths without the benefit of immersion in an explicitly spiritual culture. It is our challenge to seek the over-arching patterns that express spiritual realities and to ground them into our personal daily reality. This change may be related to the crossover from the Age of Pisces with its emphasis on the communal to the Age of Aquarius with its emphasis on the collective, which is to say coor-

---

[3]   From "Our Purpose Here", side A of *Testimony* By Ferron, Redwood Records, © Nemesis Publishing 1980

dinated individual experience. One method to attempt this challenge is to extend the old adage of "think globally and to act locally" to include the mythological and the spiritual.

The Quarters:
Elements, And Cycles Of Time

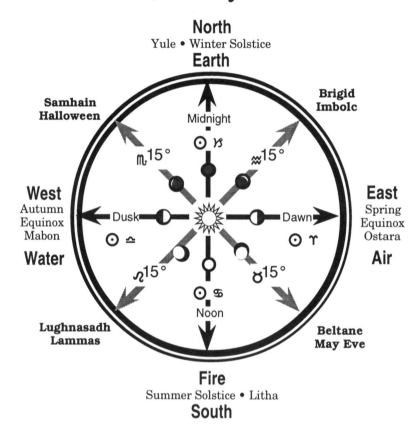

North
Yule • Winter Solstice
Earth

Samhain Halloween

Brigid Imbolc

Midnight

West
Autumn Equinox Mabon
Water

Dusk

Dawn

East
Spring Equinox Ostara
Air

Lughnasadh Lammas

Noon

Beltane May Eve

Fire
Summer Solstice • Litha
South

Charts

The charts that begin on this page provide a succinct way to view many of the Quarters' correspondences and meanings. In addition to traditional sources of lore, I have added correspondences adapted from the work of C.G. Jung that broaden the applicability of the Quarters. The Tattva symbols, though Eastern in origin are widely used in Western Magickal systems such as the Golden Dawn's, have been included as well.

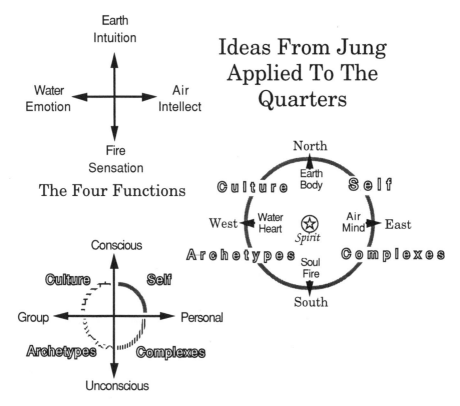

Ideas From Jung Applied To The Quarters

The Four Functions

The Division Of The Self

The Tattva Symbols
The Correlations To The Parts Of Self Are Not Traditional

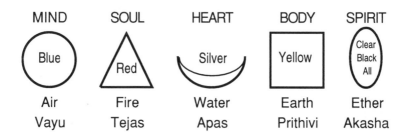

MIND	SOUL	HEART	BODY	SPIRIT
Blue	Red	Silver	Yellow	Clear Black All
Air	Fire	Water	Earth	Ether
Vayu	Tejas	Apas	Prithivi	Akasha

The Lessons Of The Elements

Magickally, there are many applications for the elements, and it is easy to become focused on the use of the elements, but it should never be forgotten that the elements are also teachers. Traditionally ascribed to the elements are the Four Powers of the Sphinx: the power to know (Air); the power to will (Fire); the power to dare (Water); the power to be silent (Earth); to which I add: the power to exist (Ether). Enfolded and encoded in the meanings of the elements and their powers are many truths and insights that lead to spiritual growth and self-realization. Since we are composed of the elements, and are surrounded by a world composed of the elements, the lessons that they have to offer are available by looking within and by looking without.

Anything that exists on the plane of matter is a combination of elements. Pure expressions of any one element do not exist. Further, any given element, through the power of ether, is forever and continually connected to every other part of itself. In other words, every fire whether it is the spark of a candle, the combustion of your metabolism, or the fusion of a distant star are all the same flame. At the same time that there are myriad manifestations—there is only one fire. In the dance of immanence and transcendence, of being and non-being, the universe is many pieces, one piece, and infinite subsets and recombinations. If the lessons of the elements are understood and their nature is fathomed the truth and the illusion of the separation between things in manifest reality is understood.

Human consciousness holds great potential because it is a melding of the four forms of consciousness described by and derived from the four elements. We are not unique in this regard, others also partake of the four-fold nature, but it is a special honor and a responsibility none the less. This becomes clear and evident in magick and in sacred space. On different planes of being we manifest in different ways. In part this is a question of subtle bodies and higher frequencies, but it is also keyed to the changes in the pattern of interaction and inter-relation between the elements as you move from plane to plane. Encounters with the Elementals, the intelligences of the Four Elements, quickly underscore our differences and our similarities.

Many Cultures, Many Quarters

The following short sections are vignettes on the Quarters from several cultures, consider them postcards that give an enticing though superficial glimpse of the possibilities.

Buddhist

When the Buddha was born a tremendous eight petaled lotus blossom rose from the earth. Remarkably, the newborn Buddha stepped into the lotus and turned to look to each of the eight directions (the Quarters and the Cross-Quarters) and then he looked up and down. To begin his life in balance he oriented himself to the ten sacred directions.

Celtic

In the Gaelic Airts the directions were associated with the path of the sun. The East was Airt and its color was the crimson of dawn. The South was Deas and its color was the white light of noon. The West was Iar and its color was the gray brown of dusk. The North was Tuath and its color was the black of midnight. The Children of the Goddess Danu, the Tuatha de Danann had four sacred cities with four sacred treasures. In the East was Gorias and the Spear of Lugh. In the South was Finias and Nuada's Sword of Light. In the West was Murias and Dagda's Cauldron. In the North was Falias and Fal the Stone of Destiny.

Christian.

In Eden there were four rivers and four gates at the four directions and at each gate stood an Archangel. These Archangels are also present at the four directions of the cross, and they are Raphael in the East, Michael in the South, Gabriel in the West, and Uriel in the North.

Egyptian

The God Horus had four sons who were born in the lotus blossom of synthesis and center. Hawk-headed Qebhsnuf was the son of Air. Jackal-headed Duamutef was the son of Fire. Human-headed Imsety was the son of Water. Ape-headed Hâpi was the son of Earth.

Greek

It is well known that the concept of the four elements undergirds much of Greek philosophy. The mythology also repeats this pattern. The Goddess Nemesis bore four sacred tools: a cup, an apple bough wand, a wheel, and a sword. The four winds were known as Eurus of the East, Notus of the South, Zephyrus of the West, and Boreas of the North.

Hindu

Before beginning, at the time of creation, the God Brahma cast his gaze to each of the four directions in preparation for his work. The Tattvas, the primal qualities of nature in Hinduism, are symbolized by: a yellow square for Earth; a silver crescent for Water; a red triangle for Fire; a blue circle (or hexagram) for Air; a black egg for Spirit.

Japanese

Shinto, the "Way of the Gods", there are four powerful guardians at each of the four directions. In the East stands Jikoku as a blue dragon. In the South stands Komoku as a red bird. In the West stands Zocho as a white tiger. In the North stands Bishamon as a black warrior. Collectively they are know as the Shi Tenno.

Judaic

The Tetragrammaton, a sacred name of God, is four letters, YHVH (יהוה). The letter Yod corresponds to the element of fire. The letter He corresponds to the element of water. The letter Vav corresponds to the element of air. The second He corresponds to the element of earth. The missing vowels that would give the accurate pronunciation of this sacred name corresponds to spirit. In its elaborated form, wherein the elements and spirit give rise to all things, the Tetragrammaton becomes the Shem ha-meforash: the 72 syllable, 216 letter, name of God.

Dineh (Navaho)

The Dineh, what the Navaho call themselves, honor the Quarters in many ways. One ritual of purification and integration involves "raising the sky" on four wands of shell, turquoise, black, and gold. The colors correspond to the aspects of Changing Woman who is: White Shell Woman in the East; Turquoise Woman in the South; Salt Woman in the West; Spider Woman in the North.

Exercises

Basic Quarters Casting

Castings, as I've defined them, are not either/or occurrences in terms of their effectiveness, but rather are on a continuum that shades from being nearly completely in everyday reality to being far into another realm of existence. The two castings that follow are warm-ups to more strenuous castings that I suggest you use as practice exercises. Although these are exercises they are still real castings and should be treated with respect. As you read more of this book and come back to these exercises they will gain more meaning and value. If you are an old hand at magickal matters, you may wish to see if the practice castings may be of value to you in any teaching work you may do.

The Quarters: Space, Time, & Elements

Preparation

Select a place indoors or outdoors where you will feel comfortable and safe to spend some time in a meditative state with your eyes shut. You will need to face each of the quarters for several minutes so if you find standing painful or difficult you may want to sit on a pillow or a chair.

Determine the directions of the place. If you do not have access to a compass you may use the Sun to set the directions. Do consider buying a compass, it's a small but worthwhile investment. For readers in the Northern Hemisphere this means that the Sun will be to the South of the zenith at noon. Near the Spring and Fall Equinoxes the rising and the setting are East and West. In the Summer the rising and the setting is North of East and North of West. In the Winter the rising and the setting will be South of East and South of West. The further North you live the greater the seasonal deviations will be. The closer you live to the equator the less variable the Sun's path. In the Southern Hemisphere the rules of thumb for the Sun's path are reversed, also correspondences need to be adjusted. Having neither lived in nor visited the Southern Hemisphere I can offer no first hand suggestions on what those adjustments may be other than proceed methodically after placing Fire, Summer, and Noon in the North. I do suggest that if you live to the south of the equator that you record and share whatever you discover with your northern neighbors.

Quarters Casting Experience I

Pick a particular set of correspondences for the Quarters such as the seasons or the elements and jot them down on an index card or a scrap of paper. You need not memorize these correspondences at this time, but at least make certain that they are familiar to you. If you like you may take this book with you into the casting. For this exercise you will also need a small container filled with water with a pinch of salt, a stick of incense, and four blue or white candles.

Considerations

• Clockwise motion is the norm in this type of casting because you are going with the direction of the Sun's path. Following the Sun's path is one way to connect with the natural flow and balance of the environment.

• The size of the circle you cast should be large enough so that you can move about comfortably, but not so large as to feel like you are not in a personal or intimate space.

• Energy flow and color visualization does not come easily for all people. One of the reasons I suggest that you use blue candles for this exercise is that they provide a source of blue to look at to help with the visualization of the casting of the circle. To help with the flow of energy you may wish to imagine warm water flowing down your arm and out your hand.

• Safety is always a consideration. Be certain that the place you selected for this exercise is secure from intrusion. You will be closing your eyes so you should be certain that the candle flames are a safe distance away from you and any flammable objects. In any case, remember the salt water that was used for purification can be used to douse flames.

• If you must leave a circle quickly, for whatever reason, and do not have time to dismiss and thank the Quarters, you should create an exit portal. To do this bring both hands together in front of you, and visualize them as glowing with blue light. Then go to the perimeter of the circle, move your hands apart as if you were parting veils and step through.

Casting Outline

I. Purification

Set aside any concerns and anxieties that are troubling you. Refer to the chapter on Inner Preparations for suggestions. After calming your mind, light the incense and feel its warmth and smell the scent. It represents the elements of air and fire. Then put down the incense or candle and dip your fingers into the container of salt water. It represents the elements of earth and water. Rub the water on your palms and put a drop on your forehead and on your lip. Feel the cool wetness and taste the salt. Feel and believe yourself to be clear, purified, and ready for entry into sacred space.

II. Grounding & Centering

Use the tree visualization presented earlier, or at the very least visualize a line of energy connecting you to the ground beneath your feet.

III. Casting The Circle

Place an unlit candle at each of the Quarters, starting in the East and progressing clockwise (East, South, West, North). Then, using your strongest hand, point at the ground and see a stream of blue fire streaming from your fingers. Starting in the East trace a circle of blue fire clockwise until you come full circle to the East once more. As you gain confidence in your energy and visualization skills begin to envision the casting of a sphere rather than a circle.

IV. Calling And Experiencing The Quarters

Light the candle in the East. Read the correspondence you selected that refers to the East, and stand or sit facing the East. Close your eyes, repeat the word "East" several times, then meditate upon the correspondence. Attend to your five basic physical senses, and any inner ones that you are aware of. What do you perceive as emanating from the East. After the images and/ or impressions, if any, have diminished allow yourself to be still and quiet before proceeding to the South. Repeat this process until you have returned to the East. If you like you may start the cycle again using different correspondences. Go to the center of the circle and experience how it feels.

Walk clockwise along the perimeter of the circle with an outstretched hand to sense the energy that marks the boundary. You may also want to shift your gaze from within to without the circle. Do you see a shimmer at the boundary or some other visual cue?

V.   Dismissing And Thanking The Quarters
When you are finished with meditating and experiencing the quarters return to the East. Thank yourself and the East for allowing an experience of its pattern and energy. Blow the candle out, imagining not that the flame is extinguished but rather that it is spread thin upon the wind. Go to each of the quarters and repeat this procedure. If you feel off balance or ungrounded touch the ground with your hand and reaffirm the line of connection.

VI.   Opening The Circle
Imagine the circle or sphere of blue fire melting away into the ground. When it is completely gone say silently or aloud: "The circle is open but unbroken". Does anything seem different now? Is the quality of the light, or the sound, or the atmosphere different after you opened the circle?

Quarters Casting Experience Exercise II

Try this casting after you have used the first exercise a few times and can remember the element, season and moon phase that corresponds to each direction. The pattern of this casting, and the previous one, is basically Neo-Pagan leaning towards Wiccan. This casting uses an invocation I wrote that references many of the correspondences as a way to remember the qualities of the direction. You may find it useful to write your own invocation as a way to personally connect with the attributes of the Quarters. In addition to the materials needed for the first Quarters casting, you will need a small mirror.

Note On Pentacles

• The pentacle, a five pointed star usually within a circle, is a magickal symbol that can be used to open or close gates between this realm and others. It represents: the four elements plus spirit; the five senses; the finite form of the human (four limbs and a head) within the circle of infinity; the five common planes of reality; and many more things. For the purpose of these exercises we will use the invoking and the banishing Pentacle of Earth (see figure below). There are many other variations but this will suffice for this purpose. Practice tracing both the invoking and the banishing versions before trying the casting. When practicing do not: move any energy, realize any blue fire, or hold the intent of actually creating a portal. For more information on Pentacles see page 66 .

The Basic Pentacle

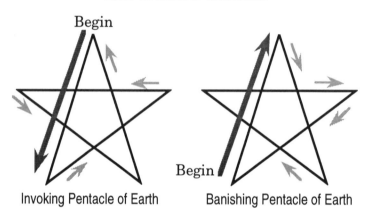

Invoking Pentacle of Earth   Banishing Pentacle of Earth

Casting Outline

I. Purification

Set aside any concerns and anxieties that are troubling you. Refer to the chapter "Inner Preparations" for suggestions. After calming your mind, light the incense and feel its warmth and smell the scent. It represents the elements of air and fire. Then put down the incense or candle and dip your fingers into the container of salt water. It represents the elements of earth and water. Rub the water on your palms and put a drop on your forehead and on your lip. Feel the cool wetness and taste the salt. Pick up the small hand mirror and gaze into your own eyes and connect with the spirit that dwells within. Imagine yourself as glowing with blue fire. Feel and believe yourself to be clear, purified, and ready for entry into sacred space.

II.   Grounding & Centering

Use the tree visualization presented earlier, or at the very least visualize a line of energy connecting you to the ground beneath your feet.

III.   Casting The Circle

Place an unlit candle at each of the Quarters, starting in the East and progressing clockwise (East, South, West, North). Then, using your strongest hand, point at the ground and see a stream of blue fire streaming from your fingers. Starting in the East trace a circle of blue fire clockwise until you come full circle to the East once more. As you gain confidence in your energy and visualization skills begin to envision the casting of a sphere rather than a circle. You may also scribe the circle (trace the connecting line of blue fire) at the same time you call the Quarters at the four gates, once you are able to attend to both actions simultaneously.

IV.   Calling And Experiencing The Quarters

As you say the invocation, make the words come to life in your inner landscape. Realize the images.

Light the candle in the East and say:

> Hail Eagles Of The East Wind Heights
> Truth Swords Of The Quicksilver Dawns
> Hail Dancers Of Yarrow Strewn Lawns
> Fleet Followers Of Sky-Clad Flights

Then, pouring blue fire through your hand, trace an invoking pentacle (see figure) in the air as you face the East. After tracing the invoking pentacle say:

> The Gate Of The East Is Open
> Blessed Be

Light the candle in the South and say:

> Hail Noon Eye, The Lady's Light Bonds
> South Brilliance Crowns The Queen Of Names
> Hail Solar Lion, Summer's Flames
> Fire Heart King Of Will And Bright Wands

Then, pouring blue fire through your hand, trace an invoking pentacle in the air as you face the East. After tracing the invoking pentacle say:

> The Gate Of The South Is Open
> Blessed Be

Castings: The Creation Of Sacred Space

Light the candle in the West and say:

> Hail Twilit Warrior Of Pearl
> Grey Dusk Prince, Autumn Cup Bearer
> Hail West Waters, Questing Seafarer
> Sail On The Sundering Sea's Furl

Then, pouring blue fire through your hand, trace an invoking pentacle in the air as you face the West. After tracing the invoking pentacle say:

> The Gate Of The West Is Open
> Blessed Be

Light the candle in the North and say:

> Hail Earth Power, Keeper Of Keys
> Bull Of Midnight, Shooting Star Ram
> Hail Dark Maiden Of Mysteries
> The North Star Of The Pentagram

Then, pouring blue fire through your hand, trace an invoking pentacle in the air as you face the North. After tracing the invoking pentacle say:

> The Gate Of The North Is Open
> Blessed Be

Go to the center of the circle and say:

> This place is sacred. I am between the Worlds.

The first few times that you do this casting you may wish to experience the quarters in a meditative way as you did in the first exercise. In subsequent castings you may wish to raise energy to see how a cast circle helps to shape and to contain energy. Energy can be raised readily by either sound or motion. You may wish to sing a series of tones rising up the scale. Don't worry if you aren't musically inclined— the point is to feel the energy not necessarily to make perfect sounds. Try making the tones saying, "Aum" which can be pronounced as "ah-oo-oh-mm" or as "ah-ohm". You may wish to walk or dance inside the circle clockwise as an act in itself or as a part of making sounds. As with most magickal acts it is intent that is vital so you must realize energy in the form of light or warmth moving through you as you chant and/or move in the circle.

Whenever energy is raised it should be for a purpose so when you are through with raising the energy release it with a visualized intent in your mind's eye. Two safe choices are personal healing or planetary healing. There is always something in need of attention or improvement in our health, and we are all deserving of healing energy. The health of our planet's biosphere is threatened and needs our help as well. I caution you against sending healing energy to another specific living being unless you have their explicit permission first. Illness is usually intertwined with the many issues of the relationship between mind, body, spirit, heart, and soul, so to intervene without permission is to intrude on the being's free will. Illness and our choices and responses to illness can be sources of insight. By asking for permission we encourage thought and insights, by acting without permission or a being's knowledge we circumvent their process and our own which can result in loss or damage Be certain that you have released the energy cleanly, completely, and if possible while holding the intent in mind. Ground and center after releasing the energy.

V. Dismissing And Thanking The Quarters

When you are finished with meditating and experiencing the quarters return to the East. Thank yourself and the East for allowing an experience of its pattern and energy. Say: "Hail and Farewell", then, pouring blue fire through your hand, trace a banishing pentacle (see figure) in the air as you face the East. Blow the candle out, imagining not that the flame is extinguished but rather that it is spread thin upon the wind. Go to each of the quarters and repeat this procedure. If you feel off balance or ungrounded touch the ground with your hand and reaffirm the line of connection.

VI. Opening The Circle

Imagine the circle or sphere of blue fire melting away into the ground. When it is completely gone say silently or aloud: "The circle is open but unbroken." [4] Does anything seem different now? Is the quality of the light, or the sound, or the atmosphere different after you opened the circle?

Follow-Up

You may wish to begin to keep a journal of your experiences with these and the subsequent castings. If you already keep a journal you may find it useful to put a star or a check mark by passages related to experiences with castings so that you can find them easily. Recording your thoughts, sensations, and feelings so that you can review them later will hasten the process of developing a sense of your personal symbols and an awareness of the states of mind that you use in sacred space. Feel free to take notes while you are in a casting if you are finding it difficult to hang on to details until you can record them.

---

[4]   Many Neo-Pagan circles end with a variation on,"The circle is open but unbroken, merry meet, and merry part, and merry meet again." The word *merry*, in addition to its common meaning, has an older meaning of *enchanted*.

More Information About Pentacles

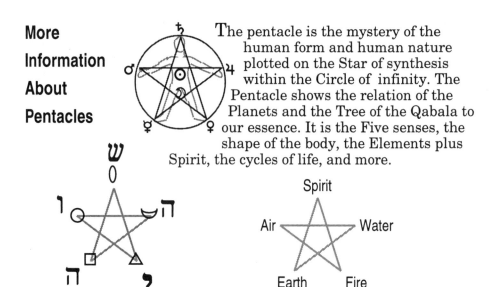

The pentacle is the mystery of the human form and human nature plotted on the Star of synthesis within the Circle of infinity. The Pentacle shows the relation of the Planets and the Tree of the Qabala to our essence. It is the Five senses, the shape of the body, the Elements plus Spirit, the cycles of life, and more.

The Hebrew Letters, Tattva Symbols, & Elements Plotted On The Pentacle

If you learn these associations you should be able to remember and understand the invoking and banishing pentacles for the Four Elements and Spirit. In most cases you may use the Earth pentacle as your universal opener and sealer of gates. There is great value in using the appropriate pentacle(s) in more elaborate rituals.

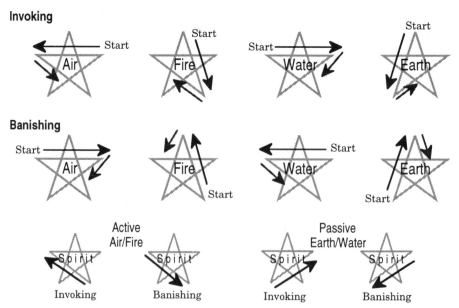

8

The Modalities & The Quarters

Introduction

Energy in the manifest universe is expressed in either the Cardinal, Fixed, or Mutable modes or as a blending of these modalities. All energy contains a certain amount of pattern or information and the Modalities describe the styles and the nuances inherent to that order. The Modalities underlie the Elemental realms and are a part of their foundations. Indeed the Modalities represent a level of order that is almost as primal as the that of Polarity. The Modalities can be likened to the quarks[1] of magick.

Although the relationships, natures, and polarities of the Elements may vary from plane to plane of existence, the pattern of relations between the Modalities remains constant from plane to plane. No matter what the frame of reference may be, Cardinal. Fixed, and Mutable follow each other in the same sequence and relate to each other in the same manner. Unlike the Elements, The Modalities do not form polarities with each other nor do they negate nor modify each other. The Modalities are the connective principle that facilitates the synthesis and the balancing of the Elements and the Planes. They are not bound into hierarchies rather they fold into each other in a recursive, egalitarian, design that shares many of the characteristics of fractal patterns.

The three Modalities may be described in only a few words, but understanding them is a different matter all together.

• The Cardinal Modality is the outpouring of energy that is creation, coming into being, assertion, and passion. In its highest expression it is the divine will to create.

• The Fixed Modality is the stabilization of energy that is rest, completion, being, and preservation. In its highest expression it is the divine will to nurture.

• The Mutable Modality is the transformation of energy that is flexibility, change, death, and rebirth. In its highest expression it is the divine will to evolve.

---

[1]   In physics, quarks are the basic building blocks for the basic particles such as electrons, protons, and neutrons. It is widely thought that you can go no smaller than quarks, but this may prove to be false.

Castings: The Creation Of Sacred Space

The Modalities have transcendent qualities as well as immanent qualities. They exist separate from each other but they also arise from each other. They can be thought of as a hybrid of states of *being* and states of *process*. In Qabalalistic terms they are a bit like the Sephiroth and a bit like the Paths The three Modalities are also related to sequences in linear time that represent the cycle of states of being that spirit encounters while sojourning in matter. To those that are conversant with Astrology, the rhythm of Cardinal-Fixed-Mutable is the natural pulse of the Zodiacal wheel (see fig. 1). Each season be-

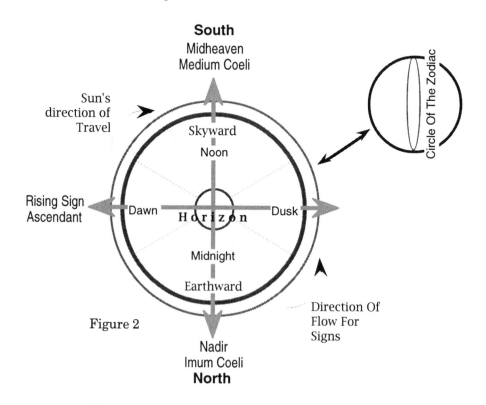

Figure 1

Figure 2

South
Midheaven
Medium Coeli

Sun's direction of Travel

Skyward
Noon

Rising Sign
Ascendant

Dawn   H o r i z o n   Dusk

Midnight

Earthward

Nadir
Imum Coeli
North

Circle Of The Zodiac

Direction Of Flow For Signs

gins in the Cardinal mode, is fully itself in the Fixed mode, and transforms to the next in the mutable mode. The Zodiacal signs can be divided into quadruplicities by their Element or triplicities by their Modality.

The Zodiacal wheel expresses the travel of the solar year and the lunar month through the Modalities, the Elements, and Signs when read clockwise. The counterclockwise flow marks the movement through the Ages. We move from the Age of Pisces to the Age of Aquarius, but from Pisces to Aries in the course of our calendar year. The cycle of Day and Night is integrated into the pattern of the Zodiac when cast into an astrological chart which anchors it to a specific place and time (see fig. 2). The Circle of the Zodiac is oriented very differently than the standard Circle of Magick. Metaphori-cally speaking they are inverted and rotated relative to each other

Figure 3

In the Circle of Magick, the Four angles in the Day/Night cycle correspond to the Four Elements and the Four Directions that are collectively referred to as the Quarters (see fig. 3). You should note that the pattern of the Modalities remains the same at the level of the Circle of Magick. As you can see the three quadruplicities and the four triplicities of the Zodiac do not plot exactly onto the Quarters. The Quartered Circle and the Zodiacal wheel though strongly interconnected operate on different levels, different planes (see fig. 4). The pulse pattern of Cardinal-Fixed-Mutable of the Zodiacal wheel repeats itself in the Quartered Circle *but* it follows the clockwise pattern of the Quarters. Another difference to take into consideration is that the standard Zodiacal wheel places East on the left hand side and normal motion is counterclockwise.

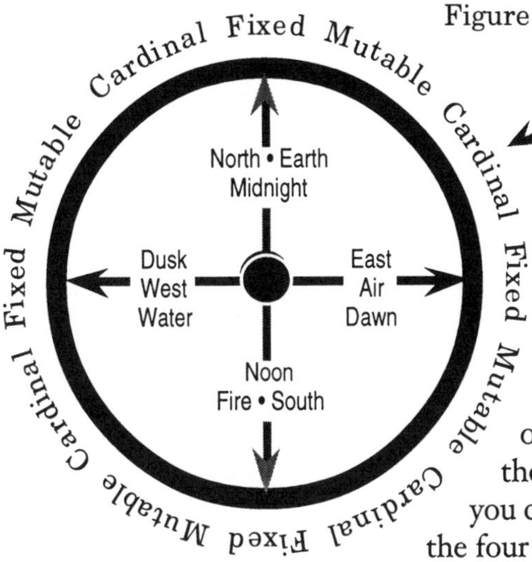

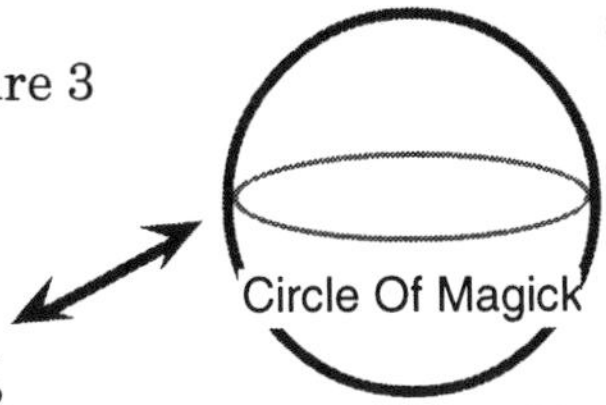

It is an esoteric truth that polarity is a relative quality that changes as we move from plane to plane. The difference between the Elemental polarities expressed by the Quartered Circle and the elemental polarities expressed by the Zodiacal wheel indicate they operate on different planes. The Elemental polarities at the Zodiacal level places the active elements as one polarity

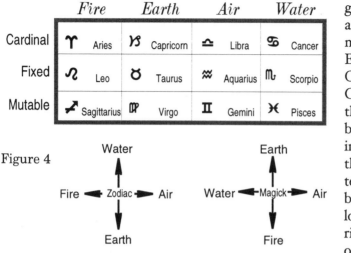

Figure 4

group (Fire/Air) and the passive elements (Water/Earth) as another. On the level of the Circle of Magick the polarities are based on contrasting the active with the passive. An interesting point to be made when looking at the polarities in the Circle of Magick is that the symbolic Great Rite of joining the Athame and the Chalice only makes sense if you assign the Element of Air to the Blade.

The Modalities And The Ages

You may notice that the Fixed modality is placed at the so-called Cardinal Directions. In the past Age of Pisces, the Cardinal Directions actually corresponded to the Mutable modality. The Cardinal Directions have not actually been *Cardinal* since the Age of Aries (roughly 2400-250 bce). It is the Sign of the Age that determines the Modality of the energy found at the Four Directions. The precession of equinoxes which governs the slow turning of the Ages has moved us into the time when the Directions correspond to the fixed modality. The Sun is now in the *constellation* of Aquarius at the Spring Equinox, a Fixed sign. This marks our passage into the Age of Aquarius. The sign of Aries is still the marker for the Spring Equinox in the Solar Year of the Zodiac.

There is a consequential distinction to be made between a constellation and a sign. The Signs in Astrology are in fact 30 degree segments of the Earth's orbit around the Sun. The twelve Signs may be seen as twelve steps in a dance describing the relationship of the Earth to the Sun. When we say we are in Aries at the Spring Equinox we have returned to the same place in the dance. The physical stars in the background that form constellations are irrelevant to the dancers— what matters is that we've returned to the same place in the music of the spheres. We can make a good guess that the esoteric science of Astrology, as we know it, was being established when the constellation of Aries was indeed the signpost in the skies for Spring. Over the millennia the Earth's position has changed so that the constellations appear to have drifted. As the earth spins on its axis producing the Day/Night cycle it also wobbles slowly with the poles tracing a circle that takes about 25,800 years to compete. The wobble slowly changes our pole star and the constellation that marks the Age. Each of the Ages takes about 2150 years and is the equivalent of a month in the Great Year. There is a chart at the end of this chapter that summarizes some of the space and time relationships in astrology.

The Modality and the Element of an Age is an important consideration for magick and ritual. The Modality of an Age sets the nature and qualities of the veils between the planes and levels of reality. The Element of the Age, and to a lesser but important degree the Zodiacal polarity of that Element, indicates the forms of magick and ritual that will have the greatest ease of functioning during that Age. It is my belief, that even though we are still in the transitional period between Ages, we have crossed far enough into the Age of Aquarius for Fixed Air to be the dominant influence. Leo in Fixed Fire is the polarity of this Age.

The Calling Of Modality Cast Circles

The Modality and Element of an Age may determine what is most easily accessible, but the other Modalities and Elements are still available. Conscious use of the Modalities offers us the potential to modify the qualities of Quarters-cast circles for specific ritual needs. Before doing so it is necessary to assess both the goal of the ritual and the normal structure of your rituals in order to see what would be most helpful. Having a personal sense of the meaning of the Modalities and a feel for their energy is a prerequisite for success in these castings. Since imagery is one of the critical elements in any magick it is recommended that you amend your call to the Quarters to include reference to the particular Modality to be used in the casting. In addition to whichever form of the invoking and banishing pentacles you use, the symbols (see fig. 5) for the Modalities that I have developed are a powerful addition to the casting. If these symbols to not speak to you on an inner level, spend some time to find your own.

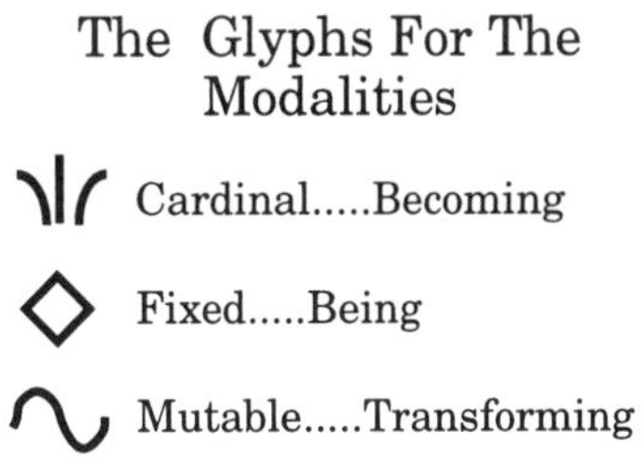

The Glyphs For The Modalities

$\mathcal{V}$ Cardinal.....Becoming

$\diamondsuit$ Fixed.....Being

$\mathcal{N}$ Mutable.....Transforming

Figure 5

Cardinal Cast Circle

The gates for the Quarters in the Cardinal Modality are found roughly 30° counterclockwise from the compass directions. (see fig. 3). If you live in an area where compasses are very inaccurate such as in the far North, far South, or near certain mineral deposits, it is better to check maps to correct the compass reading to true North. Proceed with the casting and calling of the circle in whatever is your normal protocol with whatever modifications that you have made to attune to the Cardinal Modality. Take a moment before you begin your invocation at each direction to *feel* for the Cardinal gate. Do not be alarmed by the intensity of the energy.

Fixed Cast Circle

The gates for the Quarters in the Fixed Modality are found at the regular compass directions. (see fig. 3). If you live in an area where compasses are very inaccurate such as in the far North, far South, or near certain mineral deposits, it is better to check maps to correct the compass reading to true North. Ironically this is the most difficult of the Modality castings to execute properly, especially for old hands. There is a tendency to move into the familiar headspace of calling the Directions not just the Elements. There is also a tendency to call the Elements in their undifferentiated form. Proceed with the casting and calling of the circle in whatever is your normal protocol with whatever modifications that you have made to attune to the Fixed Modality. Take a moment before you begin your invocation at each direction to *feel* for the Fixed gate.

Mutable Cast Circle

In order to cast the Quarters in the Mutable modality the call and the invoking pentacle should be made 30° clockwise from the true direction. Proceed with the casting and calling of the circle in whatever is your normal protocol with whatever modifications that you have made to attune to the Mutable Modality. Take a moment before you begin your invocation at each direction to *feel* for the Mutable gate. Do not doubt the solidity of the Mutable casting. Many interpret the changeability that is the hallmark of this energy as a weak or poorly cast circle. Examine it on its own terms and you will discern that it is strength of a different sort; flexibility does not equal weakness.

The Dismissal

The dismissal of the Modality-cast circle is comparable to any other circle using the Quarters. It is important that the dismissal make explicit reference to the Modalities. Although the consciousnesses of the Modalities are not as well defined (in human terms) as that of the Elemental Monarchs, they too merit our thanks and appreciation for their presence in our rites. I should point out a casting may be called in one modality and dismissed in another to further fine tune the impact of the casting upon the working.

Its Qualities And Uses

Most commonly a Circle is cast in the Fixed modality which is to say aligned directly with the directions of East, South, West, and North. The standard of casting in the Fixed results in a neutral sort of magickal space wherein the forces and/or entities called are not colored or modified by the casting itself but rather consolidate themselves. This is not true for a casting in the modalities of Cardinal and Mutable. In the Cardinal mode all that transpires within the circle is encouraged to assert itself, to begin anew, and to create, and/or to begin. In the Mutable mode the casting emphasizes transformation, transitions, flexibility, and the blurring and merging of forms as well as death/rebirth themes. By taking these modalities into consideration it is possible to enhance the effectiveness of a working by choosing the most appropriate energy pattern. Using the modalities is one way to make connections between the four-fold nature of the Quarters and the three-fold nature of many important deity forms or transcendent patterns.

Principles And Basis For Action

This is a casting in its purest form in that the changes in reality wrought by the casting find their source in the union of qualities and essences from different planes of reality to create a synthesis of planes. It springs from the natural flow of the slow cycle of the Ages. The foundation for the mechanism for these castings is found in the introduction to this chapter.

Limitations And Precautions

All the rules of conduct and safety that apply to Quarters-cast circles apply to those that use the Modalities. Additionally, the Modality of the Sign that the Moon occupies at the time of the ritual has a significant impact. If the Moon's place matches the Modality of the ritual, the casting will require little effort (see figures 6 & 4). If the Moon is in the Modality prior to the one of the ritual there will be some resistance. If it is in the Modality that follows the one of the ritual, then the resistance is greater still. Regardless of the Moon's Sign, this casting may be used at any time— only the difficulty varies.

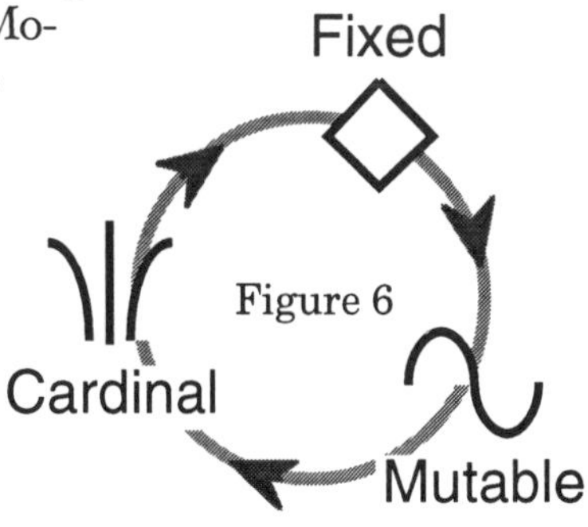

Fixed

Cardinal

Figure 6

Mutable

Castings: The Creation Of Sacred Space

Interactions With Other Castings Or Magicks

Circles cast using the Modalities have the same set of compatibilities as standard Quarters-cast circles. The variations in interactions with other magicks arise from the particular circumstances. For example: the Triangle of Stillness is compatible with this casting, but extra effort will be needed to create equilibrium because of the excess presence of one of the Modalities. I have found a lesser but similar effect with the Three Pillars. The Modality castings, other than the Fixed form, do not yield good results when combined with the Lesser Banishing Ritual of the Pentagram.

Recommendations For Mastering Its Use

Without an intimate knowledge of the Modalities these castings will fall dramatically short of their potential. Correlating the Modalities to other sets of symbols is one way to develop understanding and to access their power. In turn a deepened appreciation for the Modalities will enrich your whole body of magickal knowledge. The three-fold pattern of Cardinal, Fixed, and Mutable may be likened to other triads such as: Maiden, Mother, and Crone; Youth, Father, and Sage; Brahma, Vishnu, and Shiva; or Past, Present, and Future. The symbolic language of Astrology is perhaps the most accessible way to gain entry into this mystery, and its study could serve you well in a number of different endeavors. You may wish to examine the chapter on the Triangle of Stillness for further insights.

Meditation on the nature of the Elements and the Modalities is highly productive. Additionally, the four Elemental energy types and their various sub-elements may be multiplied by the concepts of the Modalities to yield a wide spectrum of possibilities. For example: the Fire of Water in the Cardinal mode describes, among other things, passionate desire joined with the spiritual conviction to bring new things into being. You may wish to create a listing of all the possible combinations and your interpretation of their meaning.

Advanced Form

After you have established competency and confidence in the use of the Modalities you may add additional levels to your rituals. A very effective, but taxing form of this casting, involves calling all three Modalities at each of the Quarters. This results in a circle whose perimeter is all *gate*, and allows for a large influx of energy. This version works especially well if the Astrological Signs are invoked at their station as determined by Element and Modality (see fig 4).

Conclusion

Use of the Modalities in Quarters-cast circles provides an elegant and meaningful resource for tailoring ritual space to a variety of purposes. Work with the Modalities also helps to deepen your appreciation for the mysteries of the Elements and the relationships between the planes of reality. Given the benefits compared to the relatively small learning curve, this casting is a valuable addition to anyone who uses the Quarters in their magick. If you are not already a student of Astrology, I hope that this chapter has given you the impetus to begin.

Space

60" (seconds) = 1' (minute)
60' (minutes) = 1° (degree)
30° (degrees) = 1 Sign
12 Signs = Zodiac (360°)

Time (Day)

4 minutes of time = 1° degree
2 hours of Time = 1 Sign (30°)

Time (Year)

Month = 1 Sign (30°)

Time (GreatYear)

72 years = 1° degree Precession
72 years = Great Day
2150 years = Great Month
1 Great Month = 1 Age (Aeon)
25,800 years = Great Year
Great Year = 12 Ages (Aeons)

Note:

A Great Month divided by a Great day = 29.86 which is roughly the number of days in the Lunar month. A Great Year multiplied by 81 (9 x 9) is roughly the time that the Solar System takes to orbit the Galactic Core. Nine is the number of the Moon and its magick square.

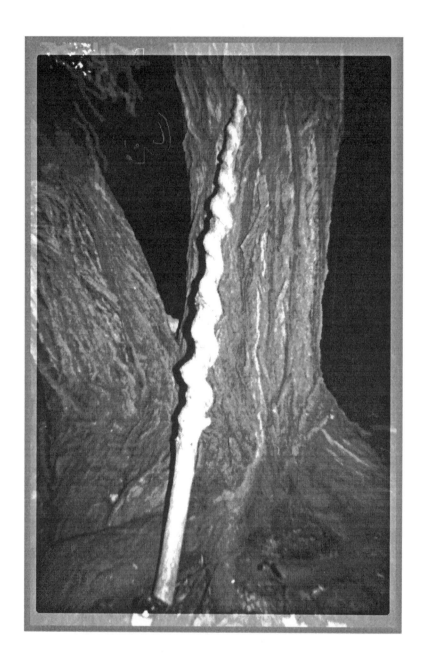

9

The Sword & Staff

Introduction

This casting creates a continually moving double vortex, often seen as a whirlpool of flames. It creates a focused pressure field of energy rather than creating a structured enclosure as do most castings. The exact shape and size of the volume affected is in continual flux throughout the duration of the Sword & Staff casting. There are large quantities of energy available to be shaped and used as needed once the casting has established its natural flow. Two objects are required for this casting: a sword and a staff, but you may substitute an athame [1] and a wand respectively. Ideally these should be consecrated magickal tools owned by the person performing the casting. In an emergency, a branch and a metal letter opener (or similar objects) may be used if they are purified and charged. Regardless of the circumstances, it is important that the Staff be made of wood and that the Sword be made of metal. The effectiveness of the casting is in part determined by the quality of the magickal tools, so given a choice use your own tools and use them consistently for this purpose.

The Calling

After grounding and centering, take a moment to check in with your emotional state and your belief in your own magickal power. Both tools should be purified immediately before being used for this casting. Salt water and incense are adequate for this purpose when combined with a flush of blue-white energy. Other methods are also acceptable so long as all Four Elements are represented in the purification. The sword (or athame) is placed on the ground with its point towards the East and hilt towards the West. For this casting either the magnetic poles or the Earth's rotational poles may be used for alignment. The staff (or wand) is then placed on top of the sword, at their midpoints, with the head of the staff pointing North and its bottom towards the South. You may experience a mild shock or sense heat when you place the staff on the sword.

---

[1]   In Wicca the athame is a sacred knife or dagger, traditionally black hilted and two edged. It has been my experience that any knife that has been consecrated and charged will do.

Though this casting will activate on its own in the presence of an incarnate soul with the intent to create sacred space, it builds up to a useful level faster if an invoking Pentacle[2] is traced over the intersection. Most techniques to call or to raise energy will also help to ignite this casting. The element of Water present within the subtle bodies of the person performing the Sword & Staff casting controls the strength and the intensity of the vortex of energy produced. Shifting your consciousness to an awareness of the power of Water within you is essential to this casting. More so than most castings, it is emotion that fuels its function.

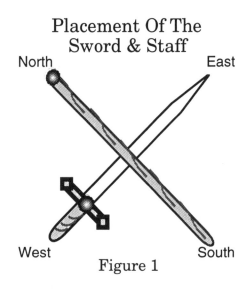

Placement Of The Sword & Staff

North

East

West

South

Figure 1

After the casting has *ignited*, stand above the intersection and use the Water qualities of your aura and your emotions to set the size, shape, and force of the casting.

This casting is always symmetrical along its vertical axis; it will reach down below you as far as it reaches above you. The edge of the casting in the horizontal plane is always changing and for brief periods may be asymmetrical. You must remain in physical contact with the vortex throughout the duration of the casting or it will collapse. You must also remain vigilant of your emotions as they will affect the vortex.

The Dismissal

Place the Sword and the Staff parallel to each other and the energy field will dissipate quickly. Although this casting loses its effect rapidly, if there is a need for a virtually instant dismissal you may stand over the intersection and reduce the force of the vortex to a minimum, and then place the tools parallel to each other. If you have the option to allow the casting to fade at its own rate, let it do so. The forces drawn together by the vortex reach some distance into the planes above and below, as well as sideways into other realms. When the casting is dismissed polarities are rebalanced to bring the motion of the vortex to rest and when this is done quickly there is the possi-

---

[2]   You may refresh your memory on pentacles by looking at the appendix or Chapter 7.

bility of a residual imbalance that could interfere with grounding and centering.

Its Qualities And Uses

Most workings and magicks that require an abundance of free flowing energy can benefit within the Sword & Staff casting. The continual motion of the vortex within the casting also allows people to tolerate higher densities, frequencies, and quantities of energy than they might normally find comfortable. Stagnant energy is unpleasant and quickly becomes unhealthy. Energy in motion, like flowing water, is cleaner and more vital. This casting responds well to chanting, motion, and other active forms of raising energy. This casting can assist in holding a large quantity of energy without having to send the energy through the aura(s) of the individual(s) involved.

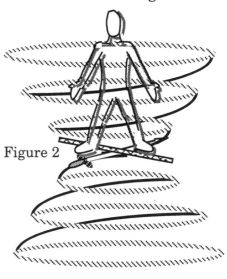

The Vortex Created By
The Casting

Figure 2

It is useful in healing work where there is an acute situation such as a recent cut, burn, broken bone, etc., or any other situation where energy is needed to repair damage or to burn away infection. It is not very effective on long standing problems such as allergies, arthritis, poor eyesight, etc., unless there is a recent change or complication. Because of this casting's ability to potentially extend far into other planes, it is useful for setting a beacon for higher assistance. It is also useful as an active defense in that you can increase the force and the direction of the flow of the vortex to push away unwanted entities or influences. You may also use the casting to return an entity to its proper place and plane or more simply to banish it. In those circumstances where active defense is needed, the Sword & Staff casting is superior to a Quarters-cast Circle when used properly.

Groups using this casting should be aware that the person who casts the Sword & Staff becomes the natural focus of energy for the duration of the casting. With proper planning this characteristic can be put to good use in focusing and sending energy. In this case the person who is the focus should be very well grounded and centered. The shape of the vortex works well with the cone of power imagery used by many Wiccan groups. With the exception of the person who cast the Sword & Staff, others may freely cross the edge of the vortex, unless they are prevented by the caster. The boundary of the vortex includes or excludes energy and entities based upon the intent and the emotion that fuels the casting.

Principles And Basis For Action

This casting is based on the active relationships and polarities between the Four Elements and between Elemental and Raith energies. The Staff is representative of Raith energies (organic subtle forces) and of Fire. The Sword is representative of Elemental energies (non-organic forces) and of Air. The "X" shaped figure formed by the intersection of the two magickal tools represents Earth, and the Cross of Matter within the circular boundary of the casting which fixes the starting point of the vortex as Malkuth [3] . The person who casts the Sword & Staff represents Water and Spirit. This casting also calls into play the polarity between Fire and Air that exists at the Zodiacal level of polarities.

The world that we live in pulses into being instant by instant as a result of the interplay of many forces and patterns, and we as incarnate beings partake of that pattern. To live, we take in matter and energy, reorganize it to suit our needs,

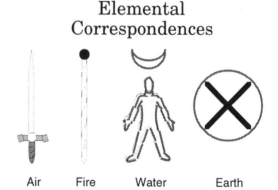

Elemental Correspondences

| Air | Fire | Water | Earth |

Figure 3

and send it out again, we also convert Elemental energy into Raith energy. In this casting, the seed pattern of living energy is used as a catalyst to create a double vortex that is analogous to our chakras. This vortex centers around the intersection of the Sword & Staff. Like a Quarters-cast Circle, the Sword & Staff casting depends upon the macrocosm/microcosm paradigm, but it is an active expression of the interface between the organic and the non-organic rather than a temple describing the static order of the Elements.

The casting draws on our archetypes and morphogenetic fields for part of

---

3   Malkuth is the Sphere of the Earth in the Qabala. It is often drawn as a quartered circle whose quarters are colored: ochre, olive, russet, and black.

its binding and ordering, the rest it draws from our incorporated knowledge. Most of the energy of the casting is derived from the environment and the polarities that it generates, but it readily accepts energy that is raised and directed towards it. Your personal Raith energy that you (and others) contribute in starting the vortex is much like priming a pump, or kick starting an engine. Once started you act as the throttle and valve for its action.

Limitations And Precautions

This casting is strongly affected by the emotional state of the person controlling the casting. If you use this casting while experiencing anger or volatile emotions you may lose control of the vortex. It is especially important that you be as centered as possible throughout the casting as you are the source for the pattern used to shape the forces that are summoned. Before attempting the casting be certain that you are at peace with the part of you that is Water and Heart. Also be ready to call forth passion and emotion because that sets the strength of the vortex.

It is the nature of this casting that only one person may participate in its creation. After the vortex of energy is established, others may help in adding strength, but the existence of the casting is rooted in the initiator. Unlike a Quarters-cast Circle, the person who casts a Sword & Staff may not leave the casting without disrupting it. They must remain in physical contact with the vortex, and indeed the vortex will stretch to try to include them. The vortex will follow the person to the limit of active energy and binding force available and then fall apart leaving only a small spark above the intersection. Anyone may dismiss the casting by following the appropriate procedure.

This casting should not be used with the Triangle of Stillness. One or both of the castings will fail and there is the potential for the Sword and/or the Staff to be damaged in a way that necessitates reconsecration and purification. Moreover when one of the castings collapses there will be a potentially harmful surge of energy, and often a small rift allowing the inappropriate passage of energy, thought forms, entities, etc. from one plane to another. Do not do this— there are safer and more effective ways to generate energy or open gates. The person who cast the Sword & Staff is most at risk of experiencing ill effects in this situation, but all those present will feel the backwash.

One last cautionary note— the vortex of energy called forth by this casting somewhat resembles the cone of power raised in many witches' circles but it is only a superficial resemblance. Do not imagine that what applies to the cone of power applies to the vortex. Two of the most important differences between the cone and the vortex are the dynamic, ever-changing, balance of polarities in the vortex and the fact that it cannot be *sent* like a cone of power.

Interactions With Other Castings Or Magicks

With the exception of the Triangle of Stillness this casting is compatible with most castings and rituals. Despite that broad compatibility, you should take into consideration if the combination is reasonable, harmonious, and befits the essence of whatever you are trying to accomplish. There can also be too much of a good thing. The Sword & Staff combined with the Triangle of Disruption, though technically compatible, results in such intense turbulence that it is exceedingly unlikely that there are any common and acceptable uses.

When used with a Quarters-cast Circle this casting is most effective when placed in the center of a Circle. In most circumstances it is best to cast the Circle first. The vortex can advance and retreat across the Circle boundary without disrupting either casting. If the vortex is not situated in the center, you may find it harder to move or shape energy in the Circle because the Sword & Staff attempts to claim the qualities of the center point.

The Three Pillars casting can be supplemented by the Sword and Staff when it is used as a technique to increase energy flow. For best results the Three Pillars should be erected prior to the Sword & Staff casting, and they should also be dismissed prior to the dismissal of the Sword & Staff casting. It can also be used when the Three Pillars are used for *rising on the planes*, but it has a smaller effect, and may prove a distraction .

Recommendations For Mastering Its Use

Self-empowerment and the acceptance of the depth of your emotions are the keys to this casting. The Sword & Staff's vortex draws its parameters (not its energy) from you. To the degree that you allow yourself to feel powerful, it will grow. For many people, the door to emotional force hinges upon trusting themselves and their emotions. In this case mastery is really about peace and trust— not raw will power. The image to contemplate for understanding this casting is not the Chariot of the Tarot with its

The Volume Affected Can Be Modified

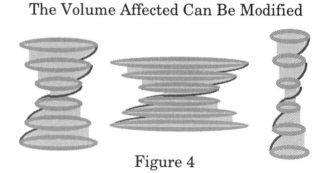

Figure 4

two contending horses held tightly in rein. The image to contemplate is that of a rider offering Pegasus soft words, apples, and a bridle of silk. You may wish to look at the chapter on "Inner Preparations" for more ideas.

Developing skill at controlling the shape of the vortex is critical to putting it to practical use. Since this is an energy pressure field very similar to a chakra, it can be manipulated with most techniques designed for working on auras, but in ritual or ceremony these may not be the most convenient approaches. The vortex's shape will respond to the physical location of its creator, and/or to their internal imagery and intent. Experiment with changing the shape of the vortex.

Please note that the figure (figure 4) , like all static drawings of moving phenomena, does not fully express the look and the feel of the vortex. Like you, it has a pulse, and though the energy is in constant motion (like your blood flow) it has a definite rhythm.

Proficiency often brings a desire to do more. If you wish to increase the intensity of the casting you may use four invoking pentacles over the intersection (see figure 5). They should be executed in this sequence: North and South then East and West.

The North and South pentacles are on the Staff and the East and West are on the Sword. Please wait until you have gained some experience with this casting before augmenting it in this way, as it is harder to control the fluctuations when the focal point covers a larger area. To dismiss the casting follow normal procedures; it is unnecessary to use four banishing pentacles. It may be necessary for you to ground more than you normally would. You may also wish to place your hands under running water to cool down your energy state.

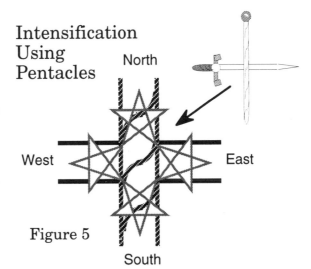

Intensification Using Pentacles

North

West

East

Figure 5

South

Conclusion

The Sword & Staff casting is highly responsive and interactive which can be a great boon or a detriment depending upon the context of its use. Of the castings presented in this book it has the potential for the highest levels of energy density. Its speed and ease of casting make it very useful for impromptu workings. It's capacity to extend far into other realms is very useful both as a way to make contact with non-physical beings and as a way to return them to their proper place. It is important to remember that within a Sword & Staff casting you are not *between the worlds* you are *through the worlds*. A secondary benefit of this casting is that it may encourage self-exploration in the realm of emotion. Self-empowerment is essential to magickal and spiritual development and making and maintaining inner peace is inextricably linked to this process.

☙IO☙

The Triangle Of Stillness

Introduction

This is a gentle and a durable casting that is valuable in and of itself, or as an adjunct to other castings or rituals. When invoked this casting creates a triangular area of stillness wherein the effects of causality and temporal forces are greatly diminished. In relative terms this means that the force of synchronicity is notably strengthened. Many report that the Triangle of Stillness feels like a pocket of the Faerie realm. This casting requires three quartz crystals in the shapes of a point, a sphere, and an egg (see figure 1). These crystals need to be of roughly the same size, color, and clarity. The crystals should be at least an inch across at their widest dimension. Prior to their use in this casting, the crystals should be purified, and ideally, dedicated to this casting. Lest you get the impression that the crystals do the work for you in this casting, I'd like to say that more than in most other types of castings, the quality and strength of this casting is dependent upon the clarity, the force, and the depth of the person invoking the Triangle. The crystals serve as anchors for the elusive forces called forth by the person casting the Triangle.

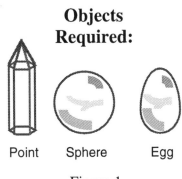

Objects Required:

Point   Sphere   Egg

Figure 1

It may be useful to read or to review the chapter on *Modalities* before attempting this casting unless you are very secure in your knowledge of the qualities of cardinal, fixed, and mutable. This casting, unlike many others, is not a binary (yes it's working, no it's not) experience, but a set of gradations into other realms of being. It expresses on a continuum from being barely detectable to being undeniable in its impact.

The Calling

Look around the place that you intend to do the casting and decide where the points of the Triangle will be located. It is important to be sure that none of the points are oriented to the four directions as determined by a compass. It is the magnetic poles, and avoiding their influence, that is crucial in this casting. Ideally, you will form an equilateral triangle, but the casting will work even if each of the sides has a different length. For your first attempt keep the size of the Triangle small, perhaps no more than 9 feet from the sides to any of the points. You may find it helpful to place three scarves, or small tables, or chairs at the points that you've selected to hold the crystals. This makes it easier to concentrate on the magick rather than on the logistics. Place the crystals, on the floor, or table, etc. as shown in figure 2.

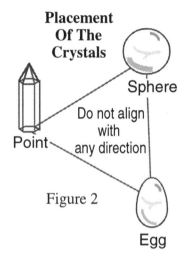

Placement Of The Crystals

Sphere

Do not align with any direction

Point

Figure 2

Egg

As always until you are comfortable with this casting feel free to bring the book into the space with you or make a copy of the one page summary from the appendix. This casting is relatively safe and forgiving in terms of its effect, and if botched it is not likely to be harmful— it just won't work. If you lose your momentum in this casting just take a moment to compose your thoughts, to ground and center, and start over from the *beginning*. You must provide the *glue* in this casting. Unlike a Quarters-cast Circle the Triangle of Stillness does not have a natural tendency towards completion. It does have a natural tendency to persist, and even after dismissal it will take some time (minutes to hours) before the area is completely returned to the prevailing qualities of the location.

When you are ready, go to the quartz point, take it in both your hands, touch it to your third eye, and then hold it aloft. Into the crystal point pour white or blue energy shaped by your understanding of:

Cardinal- the outpour, the thrust of coming into being, creation, etc.

Plus- positive polarity, pressure, increase, etc.

Past- the area of causes, the unswayable, the unalterable, etc.

After charging the crystal point, move it in an invoking pentacle. Say aloud the words, "Cardinal! Plus! Past!" When you perceive that the crystal has reached its capacity to hold energy or you have reached your limit put it down gently. You should continue to feel an energy connection to the crystal as you move on to the next crystal which is the Sphere.

Take the sphere in both your hands, touch it to your third eye, and then hold it aloft. Into the sphere pour white or blue energy shaped by your understanding of:

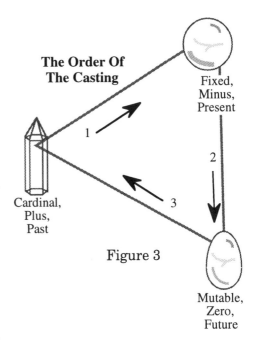

The Order Of The Casting

Fixed, Minus, Present

Cardinal, Plus, Past

Mutable, Zero, Future

Figure 3

Fixed- balance, being, preservation, homeostasis, etc.

Minus- negative polarity, suction, decrease, etc.

Present- the area of formation, the interface, the cusp, etc.

After charging the sphere, move it in an invoking pentacle. Say aloud the words, "Fixed! Minus! Present!" When you perceive that the crystal has reached its capacity to hold energy or you have reached your limit put it down gently. At this point in the casting, you should begin to notice significant changes in the feel of the space around you. You may experience it as a buzz, an echo, or definite sense of enclosure. If you are not feeling a change in the sound or the quality of light, stand where you are and send a line of energy back towards the Point and forwards to the Egg. If this doesn't work you'll need to start from the beginning. When you are ready, move on to the next crystal which is the Egg.

Take the Egg in both your hands, touch it to your third eye, and then hold it aloft. Into the sphere pour white or blue energy shaped by your understanding of:

Mutable- ending, flux, transformation, re-creation, etc.

Zero- neutral polarity, context polarity, principle of agency, etc.

Future- the area of the unformed, probabilities, possibilities, etc.

After charging the egg, move it in an invoking pentacle. Say aloud the words, "Mutable! Zero! Future!" When you perceive that the crystal has reached its capacity to hold energy or you have reached your limit put it down gently.

Then extend your psychic senses and ascertain that each crystal is radiating energy of a type consistent with its purpose and that three walls of energy have formed to give shape to the Triangle. You may safely add energy to any part that seems dimmed, but generally this is not needed. If the perimeter walls do firm up, add a scribing of the Triangle to the protocol of the casting. The Triangle of Stillness is complete. This is the simplest, but by no means the only, way to cast a Triangle of Stillness. It may be done as solo or as a group effort. Because consistency of energy is essential to success, a focal person is recommended in group efforts. So long as the essence of the casting stays constant it may be embellished and modified to fit the needs of a given ritual or Tradition. However, it is best to gain proficiency in the basic config- uration of the Triangle before experimenting with all its possibilities. One of the easiest modifications you can make is the use of an invocation at each of the three crystals not unlike what is done at the Quarters in casting a circle.

This is an example of a more elaborate invocation that can be used in this casting:

> Aries, Cancer, Libra, Capricorn!
> > Celestial Bearers Of The Cardinal Force Join Us In This Rite.
> Ancient Of Days, Mother Of Time
> > Let The Power Flow From The Headwaters Of The Past!
> By The Law Of Polarity
> > Let Positive Seek Negative.

> Taurus, Leo, Scorpio, Aquarius!
> > Celestial Bearers Of The Fixed Force Join Us In This Rite.
> Mother, Ever-Birthing The World, Lord Of The Dancing Moment
> > Guard The Perfection Of The Present!
> By The Law Of Polarity
> > Let Negative Return To Zero.

> Gemini, Virgo, Sagittarius, Pisces!
> > Celestial Bearers Of The Mutable Force Join Us In This Rite.
> Dreaming Ones, Weaving Ones, Bright Child Unborn
> > Bring From Eternity The Promise Of The Future!
> By The Law Of Polarity
> > Let Zero Find The Mystery Of Beginnings.

The Dismissal

To dismiss the Triangle go to the Point and withdraw the energy that you called into the crystal. Hold it the same way that you did when you cast the Triangle. Let the energy drain through you and be grounded by the earth beneath your feet. If you are able, try to make a distinction between information and energy in closing down the crystals. If you intend to use the same set of crystals for this casting regularly, it's best to leave the pattern of the casting embedded in the crystals so as to strengthen future efforts. For this reason, it is best not to use banishing pentacles as a part of the dismissal.

Go to the Sphere repeat the same procedure, and then the Egg. As I indicated earlier, this casting tends to linger after dismissal. If there is an urgent need to return the area to its normal state you can speed up the process. After withdrawing the energy from each crystal place it in a pouch or other suitable container, so that the three are in physical contact with each other. Then send the three lines (or walls) of the Triangle into the earth.

Its Qualities And Uses

The Triangle of Stillness does not create the type of firm boundary that is called forth in a Quarters-cast Circle. The intensity of the effect is evenly felt within the Triangle, and the boundary fades out a little bit past the crystals (see figure 4). The Triangles are not disrupted by passage through their boundaries. This property makes the Triangle useful in those situations where people will be entering and leaving the space without regard to the presence of a casting. One of the Priestesses in my coven wanted to give birth within sacred space but within the walls of a hospital.

She used a Triangle of Stillness because it was durable, created the serene space she desired, and was impervious to the many comings and goings of the nurses, friends and doctors. Additionally, the Triangle of Stillness has a special relationship to the 32nd path of the Qabala that correlates to the birth passage. Any magickal or spiritual work that hinges on a balancing of forces resulting in a lessening of polarity, linear time, and causality may benefit from this casting.

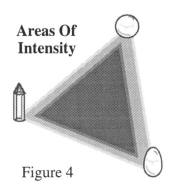

Areas Of Intensity

Figure 4

Some Recommended Uses

Meditation- This casting tends to hush or muffle the clamor of inner voices which often interfere with meditation. It is also very good for finding your still center point within because of the resonance and reinforcement of existing balances that the Triangle calls into play. Psychologically and psychically the Triangle feels comforting and nurturing.

Counseling- The broadening of the temporal focus allows for memories from different time periods to meet and interact on a flat field. The subjective experience of the present is not a point in a Triangle but an area. The increase in the effect of synchronicity encourages discovery, grace, and serendipity.

Healing- Although most types of healing work can be assisted by the use of this casting, those that involve chronic conditions will find the most improvement. The combination of reduced causality and greater flexibility in the flow of time work well on long-standing illnesses or injuries.

Divination- All forms of divination that derive a good portion of their function from the psychic and intuitive activity of their practitioner are improved within a Triangle of Stillness. Divinatory techniques that are based more on linear thought are not helped by the Triangle. For example, Tarot or Scrying benefit greatly in a Triangle whereas Astrological analysis would not benefit much. Of course different practitioners rely to different degrees upon their talents so this is not a hard and fast rule.

Qabala- The Triangle resonates to the Sephiroth of Yesod, Hod, Netzach, and all their related Paths. Moreover it contains the mystery of the space enclosed by the triangle formed by those Sephiroth and their Paths. Traditionally, Qabalistic workings concern themselves with the Spheres and the Paths; this working uses the volumes delineated by the Tree as well. It can be used to enhance workings or meditations on any part or the Qabala as a whole but it is best suited to the Sephiroth indicated.

Principles And Basis For Action

This casting calls upon three sets of three generating a 3 | 9 pattern that evokes the forces that underlie and overlight the plane of matter. Numbers are in many ways the purest expression of the Universe's structure. The number three is the concept or essence of form and 9 is its elaboration into the actual. The 3 | 9 pattern relates to the connection between Binah and Yesod. Binah equilibrates the influence of Yesod and their associated numbers are 3 and 9 respectively. The three process states of being (modalities), the three primary polarities, and the three temporal states are part of the foundation that supports the realms of the Elements and the realm that we live in. The Triangle of Stillness summons and brings into focus those powers that are enfolded into the web that sustains not only the lower planes but is the lower reflection of those powers that undergird higher realities. That is why the Triangle should not be aligned to the Four Directions, as that would drag the casting towards the influence of the Elements. The calling of the Nine: Cardinal, Fixed, Mutable; Plus, Minus, Zero; Past, Present, Future, produces a dynamic balance that stills external forces within the Triangle.

Limitations And Precautions

This casting is completely incompatible with the Sword & Staff casting. When cast together, in any combination, one or the other will fail. Moreover when one of the castings collapses there will be a potentially harmful surge of energy, and often a small rift allowing the inappropriate passage of energy, thought forms, entities, etc. from one plane to another. ***Do not do this —*** there are safer and more effective ways to generate energy or open gates. Additionally, if it is the Sword & Staff casting that fails, either or both of the tools will need to be reconsecrated, charged, and possibly mended.

Do not sleep or spend extended periods within the Triangle of Stillness unless you are looking for the psychic equivalent of jet lag. The length of time varies for individuals and is also dependent upon the strength of the casting, but as a general rule do not stay in the Triangle more than 3-5 hours. Stillness and balance are good things, but our physical and subtle bodies also need catabolic action to remain healthy and energized. When you sleep, various parts of your self travel away from your physical form. Going into a deep sleep or dream sleep state while inside a Triangle of Stillness could make it harder for you to refocus and rebalance after awakening and leaving the Triangle. Should this happen to you, grounding and centering will help, but time is the best remedy.

The size of the Triangle that you can effectively cast is limited by the size of the crystals used. When you've developed skill and stamina you should be able to cast a Triangle up to about 19 feet across from base to vertex. Beyond this size the crystals need to increase about an inch in size for every 9 feet. Additional people providing energy will intensify the casting but not its size. The crystals act as anchors to hold the balance of the casting. Consider the metaphor of an anchor; a small anchor will not hold a large ship in place.

If you do not have the needed crystals but you have three talented people willing to act as the anchors you may cast the Triangle using them. They must for the duration of the casting remain at their point and call forth the appropriate energy. The Triangle should not be over 19 feet if you are using living anchors. Special attention should be given to grounding and centering for the anchors after the casting, and if the knowledge is available their chakras should be balanced.

If the Triangle is to be used in combination with any other casting it is important that the size of the castings stays constant throughout the working or ritual. For many people it is an acceptable practice to expand a Circle, by adding energy to its perimeter, after it has been cast if the space feels cramped. This does not work well in combination with the Triangle, which will often dissipate if its size is changed. Take the number of people participating in ritual and the space you have available into consideration before beginning this casting.

Interactions With Other Castings Or Magicks

Experience and logic will be your best guide to how to combine the Triangle of Stillness with other castings or ritual elements, but there are a few things that I'd like to share from my experiments. When combined with a Quarters-cast Circle the results vary depending upon whether the Triangle is within the circle or surrounding it. When the Triangle is inside the perimeter of the Circle it helps to create an environment conducive to the presence of energies and entities that normally find it difficult to remain on this level of existence. In this configuration the perimeter of the circle retains its protective qualities. If the Triangle surrounds the Circle, the space enclosed by the castings does not serve as a barrier to intrusion, but it does have the property of being easily moved through the various planes of reality, so serves as a good vehicle for rising on the planes.

The Triangle casting responds to local defined conditions so that if you are combining it with a casting or a ritual that creates a specific coordinate system or pattern that identifies axes or directions make sure that none of the points of the Triangle line up with the structure. This is an extension of the prohibition against aligning the points to any of the Four Directions. If for some reason this is unavoidable you'll find that the effectiveness of the Triangle is hampered.

The Triangle is very compatible with most Shamanic practices, with the exception of dancing your power animals. Indeed any physically active working is not helped by the Triangle of Stillness. Entry to and return from the otherworlds is eased by this casting. The only special consideration in this regard is to make a specific symbolic act that closes the gates after you have completed your journey. Since the Triangle fades slowly after dismissal you may have unwanted visitors if you don't close the gates.

The Triangle can be used in direct conjunction with Goddess or God forms so long as they have a triune nature that maps onto the 3 | 9 pattern of this casting. The Maid, Mother, & Crone, or Brahma, Vishnu, & Shiva are examples of the types of sets that work readily, but there are many other possibilities. The peace and balance that the Triangle of Stillness fosters is well suited to devotional activities. Often triune deity forms are complicated and can be correlated to the qualities of the Point, Sphere, and Egg in more than one way. Be certain that the correlations that you choose make sense within the context of the particular purpose of that specific working or ceremony.

Recommendations For Mastering Its Use

Many people find it easier to call forth qualities and energy through the use of symbols. I have a set of symbols that I use for the quick notation of the process states of being (modalities), the primary polarities, and the temporal states that you may wish to use in meditations as a part of your preparation to casting the Triangle. You may also wish to trace and charge these symbols during the casting in the same way that you would use invoking Pentacles in other castings (see figures 5 & 6). The color of the energy used in tracing the symbols should be either blue, white, or if for some reason you're using different colors for the sake of the ritual at hand, make the colors consistent.

You may wish to ask yourself these questions and meditate on the answers that you find as a way to master this casting.

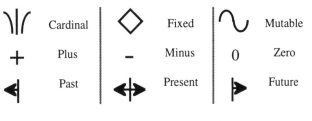

The Symbols Charged At Each Point

Cardinal	Fixed	Mutable
Plus	Minus	Zero
Past	Present	Future

Figure 5

- Do you truly and deeply understand the qualities of:
- Cardinal, Fixed, & Mutable | Plus, Minus, & Zero | Past, Present, & Future
- Do you understand why and how the three sets of three interrelate as: groupings for this casting?
  Cardinal, Fixed, & Mutable | Plus, Minus, & Zero | Past, Present, & Future
- Do you understand the shapes of the crystals in relation to the casting and the qualities called?
- Numerologically what is implied by a 3 | 9 pattern?
- Can you call up these qualities and energies within yourself in an emotional and a somatic manner as well as a mental manner?
- As in all castings, can and do you approach the invocation of the Triangle of Stillness with reverence, awe, or other stances appropriate to the creation of sacred space?

Conclusion

The Triangle of Stillness creates a space sheltered from the flux and the turbulence of causal and temporal forces, and as such has many potential spiritual and magickal uses. If its limits are respected, the Triangle is a casting that can be incorporated into a wide range of ritual forms. It is also one of the few truly durable castings whose boudaries may be crossed repeatedly without incident. In and of itself the Triangle of Stillness can be done very simply or elaborated into Ceremonial High Magick.

**The Symbols
And The
Crystals**

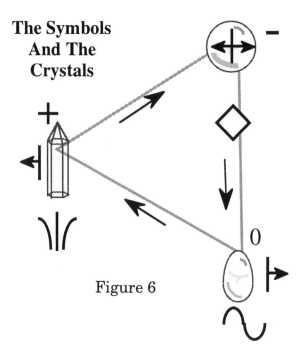

Figure 6

The Square Of Abeyance

Introduction

This casting creates a volume in three dimensional space wherein energy patterns and frequencies that are not native to the physical plane of reality are made null and void if the casting is taken to its fullest power. Additionally, those energy patterns and frequencies that are the natural links between planes are damped but not extinguished. Since the casting is created by an incarnate human, the vibrations needed for life and the cohesion of the subtle bodies and spiritual forms are not affected, but those energies that link beings psychically are virtually shut down. Depending upon their nature, non-physical forms and energies are held in abeyance which may result in stasis, dismissal, or dissolution. This casting is neither selective nor perceptive in its impact on non-physical beings as are some other castings; all are excluded whether desired or not. This means that spirit guides are just as likely to be excluded as are poltergeists.

The Calling

Choose the size of the area that will be affected, taking into consideration anything that is magickally fragile or that you do not wish to dismiss. As with most castings it is a volume that is enclosed not just a flat representation. Unless altered by conscious intent, the Square produces a rectangular space about a head taller than the tallest person enclosed by the casting. To be more exact, the Square's natural tendency is to form its perimeter just below the transpersonal chakra [1] of the tallest person. If the person creating the Square is not enclosed within the intended volume the casting is substantially more difficult to call into being but it can be done. The person constructing the Square must create a sphere of energy invested with some portion of their consciousness to float above the casting.

To begin the casting create a line of matte black energy from the North to the South of the midpoints of the Square (see figure 1). The energy should be

---

[1]   See the appendix on Chakras if you are unfamiliar with the transpersonal chakra. This is the chakra that floats above the crown chakra and can be correlated to the *personal Kether*.

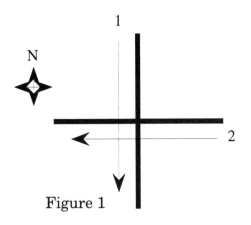

Figure 1

as passive, receptive, and absorptive as you can manage. Then create another line of matte black energy from the East to the West to form an equal arm cross. Visually survey your work to make sure that it is symmetrical.

Enclose the equal arm cross in a square outline of matte black energy (see figure 2). You may do this in whatever pattern of visualization works best for you. The most important consideration is that the square be properly aligned with the equal arm cross. If you are able it is better to to draw the square starting in the North and proceeding clockwise until you return to the North point once more. Although results are better if the square is drawn in this manner it is more important that you choose the method of visualization that best suits you. If your skills at drafting with the inner eye are a bit weak there is no harm in using a few pieces of tape or a few chalk marks on the floor as helpers. If you do use tape or chalk choose black, white, or gray or else you will ruin the casting if you are distracted by a splash of color.

Starting in the North-East quadrant fill the square (see figures 2 & 3). You are actually creating a rectangular solid with the gray energy of active neutrality, but the flat representa-

4	1
3	2

Figure 2

tion is adequate for its formation. This gray energy may be compared to the static of a radio or a television tuned to a missing station. It is like white noise in that it contains many frequencies, but in no particular pattern. It is neutral in its flux and indecision rather than in being an average or in being indefinite. It is active in that it is continually changing but it does not engage or interact with other energies. White may be thought of as the blending of all colors in harmony or the reflection

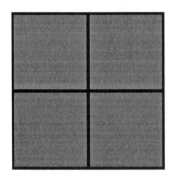

Figure 3

of all light equally. Black may be thought of as the absence of all colors or the absorption of all light equally. The gray of active neutrality is like a froth or a foam of white and black, continually changing as bubbles of white or black form and disperse randomly. On a micro-level there is great irregularity and variation in shades of gray, and on a macro-level it appears as a shimmering gray.

After filling the remaining quadrants with gray energy in clockwise order, examine the entire square carefully. If necessary, add energy until the entire square has a homogeneous density. When you are satisfied, will away the matte black square and equal arm cross (see figure 4).

Figure 4

The matte black energy should either be grounded or dissolved into the gray. Once again visually survey the casting looking for any traces of matte black or areas that are not completely uniform. The Square of Abeyance is now complete (see figure 5).

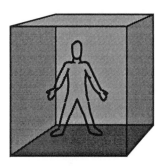

Figure 5

The Dismissal

The person who cast the Square need only introduce a spark of energy of any bright, ideally prismatic, color into the gray and the casting will fade away. The spark of color is like a crystal introduced into a super-saturated solution, it provides a model of order that triggers the growth of pattern. The Square fills with color then the energy falls into train with rhythm, patterns, and colors of local energies. The dispersal of this casting is very swift. With the Square of Abeyance it is possible for the maker to leave the Square after it has been cast and to dismiss it from a distance. It is difficult, but not impossible for someone other than the maker to dismiss this casting, because the gray energy of active neutrality (in this casting) derives its flux pattern from the random variations that naturally occur in the physical and sub-etheric levels of the caster. If it is your intent to have more than one person in command of this casting then it must be cast jointly. Success in a joint casting is improbable unless the parties involved have had practice in blending their energies together evenly.

Its Qualities And Uses

At first glance you may wonder why anyone would want to create a volume wherein the limits of the Earth plane are maximized, but there are many valid uses for this casting. If there is a home or a room in a home where there are unpleasant emotions or energies that are lingering and have been resistant to being cleared, the Square of Abeyance can dispel the unwanted presence. If a person believes themselves to be under psychic attack or affected by a curse, an exceedingly rare situation, then the Square may be used in several ways. If the person reports no change within the casting, then it is probable that what they are experiencing is self-generated. If they feel relief then there is the possibility that their discomfort is caused by an external source, but there is also the possibility that the discomfort was illusory in the first place and that the casting has acted as a placebo.Given that warning, the Square when used with discernment can act as a touchstone to determine the presence or absence of baneful magic or unhealthy psychism. Further in most cases, time spent within a Square of Abeyance is generally enough to undo the bindings of a curse or to provide a sufficient respite to reestablish shields against psychic intrusion. The Square may also be used to free objects, such as jewelry or tools, from the energy and pattern of its previous owner. Depending upon the strength of cohesion of the energy impression in the object this may take hours or days. There are also uses for this casting in specialized and advanced forms of healing that with some thought should become apparent to those ready to undertake such serious work.

Principles And Basis For Action

The matte black equal arm cross resonates to the limiting structuring power of Binah [2] and its lower reflection in Malkuth as well as the cross of matter in its densest form. The Four Directions addressed as *Quadrants* speaks to the elements and their sub-elements as a static affirmation of existence rather than as a call to directed action. The Quadrants are the Elements in their unmanifest form through which they underlie and stabilize the plane of matter. The black boundaries maintain balance by holding apart polarities until they are neutralized by the gray energy. The gray energy of active neutrality favors entropy, an increase in disorganization, therefore nonliving or non-ensouled energy patterns tend to disperse. The capacity to resist entropy and to increase order is one of the hallmarks of living energy or living beings. The sum of the influences in this casting also makes it difficult for non-physical beings to remain on or near the Earth Plane because the casting disengages the levels used by entities to drop anchor or attach to a place in

---

[2]   See the appendix on the Qabala for more information

linear space-time. To continue the metaphor it also reduces friction and viscosity so that even treading water to stay in our plane is virtually impossible. Lastly it is a highly unpleasant environment for non-physical beings. Imagine your reaction to random noise and stray signals running through the full range and gamut of your sensory perception capabilities. The power of this sensory overload is commensurate with the quantity and the intensity of the energy put into the casting.

Limitations And Precautions

The Square of Abeyance can neither be cast nor made to extend beyond the plane of the Earth nor the planes that are one step short away from physical. The Square does not extend into the Elemental realms. You may not cast the Square on the Astral to shield yourself from some unpleasantry. It simply will not work, and it will distract you from taking more appropriate action. Attempting to cast the Square on other planes will make you highly visible to any other beings, human or otherwise, that are on the plane at that time. It creates an energy disturbance whose ripples can be perceived by many beings at significant distance, and whose ripples provide a traceable homing beacon for any who are curious. Furthermore the attempt will probably obscure your vision and perception on other planes as it is difficult to see through the gray energy.

The Square disrupts most other castings including Quarters-cast circles, the Triangles, and the Sword & Staff. It may be no great problem to avoid using this casting in combination with others, but in the case of sacred space that is a temple room or a grove it may pose a problem. This casting cannot undo what nature has done as in the case of ground that is sanctified and empowered by ley lines, vortices, devas, etc. It can however disrupt the connection between the physical anchor of a temple, nemeton, or ritual space, that has been created by humans, and the astral forms that have been built up unless the power and cohesion of the space is quite strong. In that case what results is stasis, rather than disruption, until the casting is dismissed. The same warning applies for any spells or workings that may be enclosed inside the Square, and generally speaking they are fragile.

Magickal tools or objects are safe from harm so long as they are in contact with your physical or etheric body. So that a ring, a pendant, or a wand in your hand would suffer no change in its qualities other than being inert for the duration of the casting. But a tarot deck or an athame on a table within the Square of Abeyance would begin to lose their charge and energy patterning with that which is newest, or most recently impressed upon them, being lost first.

Interactions With Other Castings Or Magicks

I am unaware of any castings that are compatible with the Square of Abeyance, and experimentation is likely to produces losses and unwanted results.

Nonetheless, should you choose to experiment, please be prudent and cautious in your efforts, and take copious notes. It is not my field of expertise, but it is possible that some forms of Chaos magick could be augmented by the use of the Square. There may also be Enochian workings that could make use of the Square. but again— I am uncertain.

The Square does not undo or damage any magick that is an integral or incorporated part of a person's energy field. Initiations, healings, and other workings that behave in a coherent and congruent manner relative to the structures in a person's aura are unaffected. Magick that is of a superficial nature may be weakened or stripped away completely. For example spells of illusion, glamours, and so on would be affected.

Recommendations For Mastering Its Use

Mastering the Square is a question of gaining sufficient focus and concentration to avoid the unwanted stray thought that interrupts the casting by adding color or order to what should be virtually chaotic. It is also a test of whether or not the inner voices of doubt and self-sabotage can be quelled for the duration of the casting. One spark of energy of any color and the casting disperses. It's like telling someone not to think of pink elephants, the image almost leaps to mind immediately.

It is common for people to have difficulty in increasing the power and intensity of this casting. In most cases when energy is raised, channeled, or shaped it has a specific color or vibration and most people use that specificity as the handle or as the measure for the energy. This casting requires the raising of energy that lacks the familiar attributes that are generally linked to the tags or internal markers that people generally use when working with energy. One suggestion to overcome this stumbling block is to experiment with different rhythms of breath to gather and to control energy. Another is to focus on experiencing the energy as motion, pressure, and temperature rather than as color or light.

The Square of Abeyance is not a casting that most people are drawn to for the joy of the experience so it is easy to avoid practicing this casting until it is absolutely needed. Given the purposes that the casting is best suited for, it would be unwise to wait until that time. It should be remembered that the casting can be practiced without being inside the Square. Also, working with the gray energy of active neutrality is good practice and can be done without doing the casting.

Conclusions

The Square of Abeyance is unique among the castings in this book as it offers contra-magick. It is contra-magick because it limits, binds, or diminishes the impact of the subtle energies and subtle planes on ours. Though shelter from subtle energies and from non-physical beings is afforded by other castings, the Square does so by nullification rather than shielding. Its potential for use in purification and exorcism is considerable. It must be used with caution lest there be inadvertent harm done to magickal objects, beings, and workings. Its use and mastery is useful in developing mental discipline which is a beneficial side-effect. It is not compatible with most castings or magicks, but since it is a very sharp edged, well defined volume that is affected some advanced combinations are possible.

⚡12⚡

The Three Pillars

Introduction

The basis for this casting is rooted primarily in the powerful construct known as the Qabala or the Tree of Life. It is not necessary that you be conversant in the lore of the Qabala in order to make use of this casting, but your effectiveness in using the Three Pillars will increase if you have incorporated that knowledge into yourself. This casting also resonates to the construct of three main nadis [1] of the Chakra system: Ida, Pingala and Sushumna. In fact, affinities between the Three Pillars and many other magickal patterns based on triune nature abound. This casting relies upon correlations to metaphysical structures inherent in the foundations of reality as well as to thought structures created by human belief in order achieve its stability and cohesion. However, this casting does not build upon itself. Many castings have *a life of their own*— once they come into being they have a tendency to be self-sustaining but the Three Pillars do not. The Three Pillars need to be fed energy throughout the duration of the casting or they will lose resolution and fade out. Because of their resonant link to various morphogenetic and metaphysical patterns there is a certain amount of momentum and inertia transferred to the Three Pillars so that the energy feed need not be constant, only consistent.

Not surprisingly, there are three primary ways to execute this casting. The Three Pillars may be cast externally, internally, or microcosmically depending upon the effect desired. The external variant most resembles the other castings in this book. The other two are hybrid forms that also resemble meditation or energy working techniques. *Externalized*, the Three Pillars produce a triangular shaft that greatly facilitates movement up or down through the planes of reality. Those within the shaft are shielded against many of the stresses of such travel. *Internalized*, the Three Pillars greatly augment the capacity of the person who has received the Pillars to conduct energy and information through their central core. The person's resistance to being a con-

---

[1] The nadis are channels in the subtle bodies that share some of the properties of both nerves and blood vessels.

duit is greatly lessened by the addition of temporary channels to spread the load. When cast *Microcosmically*, the person generating the casting becomes a focal consciousness for manifestation or the rebalancing of energy between planes (see figure 1). With care and practice they can work in coordination with land spirits, devas, and other beings in healing and co-creating.

Externalized	Internalized	Microcosmically

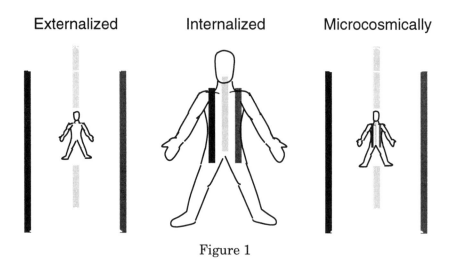

Figure 1

Background

In order to cast the Three Pillars it is necessary to grasp some of the associated sets of three that make up the ordering principles of this casting. This casting also brings to mind the Triangle of Stillness in that the caster must call the primal properties forth from themselves. It is yet another way of accessing the power of the microcosm/macrocosm polarity. The dynamic tension between the Small and the Large gives this casting most of its power. Like calling the powers of the elements, calling the Three Pillars into your presence is also an affirmation of the underlying structures of the universe. What the Three Pillars lack in natural stability of cohesion is more than compensated for by the increased accessibility of energy and the reduction in resistance to traversing the veils that they provide.

Although not absolutely necessary, I strongly recommend that you take time to learn the rudiments of the Qabalah. At the very least spend time meditating on the sets of associations presented in Figure 2. When you feel that you have achieved some depth of understanding of each set of associations, see if you can generate further sets of three. When you feel confident in your understanding of the relationships between these associations then

Some Pillar Associations

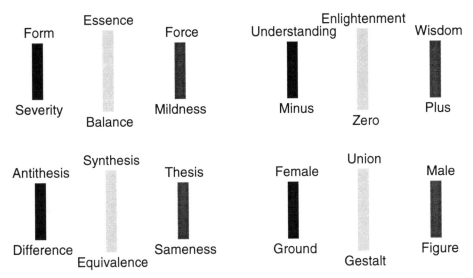

Figure 2

you may proceed with learning the protocols for this casting. If you do not invest the time needed to become properly attuned to these governing principles there are significant risks. This casting allows you to exceed your normal limits and capacities so if it fails you may find yourself out of your depth and in danger. It may be well to mediate on the Tower of the Tarot's major arcana.

The Calling

All three forms of this casting depend upon the creation of three energy constructs in the form of the Three Pillars. The first Pillar is made of brilliant diamond fire and is the middle pillar of equilibrium. The second Pillar is made of sapphire blue fire and is the pillar of force. The third Pillar is made of ruby red fire and is the pillar of form. This is the order in which the pillars are created for use in this casting, tracing a deosil triangle. You may visualize the Three Pillars as simple cylinders, as ornate Corinthian columns, or however else you please so long as they remain identifiable as pillars (see Fig 3).

The colors are very important in this casting. It is not adequate to imagine bright white, blue, and red to bring forth the energy needed to create the Pillars. The beautiful purity of the jewel tones of diamond, sapphire, and ruby must be evoked. The play of light and fire in those gems is part of the power of this casting. You may wish to go to a jeweler or to a gem and mineral show to firmly implant the look and the feel of these stones in your mind.

The externalized form of the casting requires pillars that are at least a head taller than the tallest person present. The internalized form requires pillars that would fit from the bottom of the spine to the nape of the neck. The microcosmically cast form uses one large set and one small set of pillars. In the case of the internalized *and* the microcosmically cast forms, each individual must create their own pillars. The externalized form may be shared easily; passage through the perimeter marked by the Three Pillars does not disrupt the casting so long as energy is provided to maintain focus.

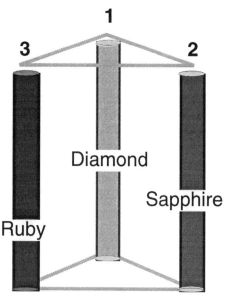

Figure 3

Each Pillar begins with the circle of its base scribed with energy the color of the appropriate gem (see figure 4). Then the circle is quartered with two lines of energy forming an equal-arm cross. Another circle is scribed over the first and an invoking pentacle of earth is placed within it. If it is your custom, use the sixth sealing stroke in making the invoking pentacle. Make the circle with the star rise to the height needed for the casting. The height is determined by the form the casting will take. As it rises, imagine the Pillar forming and filling with energy. If the Pillar looks dim or is wavering feed it more energy through the base. If the height of a Pillar needs adjustment, see the pentacle blaze with fire the color of the Pillar and move it up or down. Each of the Pillars is created in this manner.

When the Pillars are complete, beginning with the Diamond Pillar, draw a veil of rainbow fire from it to Sapphire, and then to Ruby, and back to Diamond. The veil should run the complete height of each Pillar. This step in the casting may be completely mental, but is better accomplished with gestures and motion. This is especially true if this casting is to be used in group ritual, and is al-

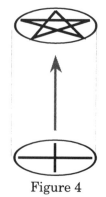

Figure 4

most an imperative if all are lending energy to the veil. Rainbow fire has the transparency of a physical rainbow but with the quick, flickering, changeability of flames. As with the Pillars, you may need to add energy to the veil after the initial casting. The veil is one unit so adding energy to any part of it will reinforce the whole.

Summary Of The Externalized Form
Three Pillars are cast in a triangle enclosing all that are involved in the working. The Pillars should be taller than the tallest person in the group.

Summary Of The Internalized Form
Three Pillars are cast around the body within the etheric [2] layer of the aura. The Pillars should rise from the level of the base of the spine to the level of the nape of the neck. This cannot be used as group working though various individuals within the ritual space may create their own.

Summary Of The Microcosmic Form
Three Pillars are cast externally and then they are cast internally. This cannot be done as a collective working though a single individual within a group may use this casting as a part of a larger ritual.

The Dismissal
The pillars should be dismissed in the same order as they were cast, Diamond, Sapphire, Ruby, and they should be dismissed one at a time. First, the pentacle at the top and the equal-arm cross at the bottom of the Pillar should be erased. When the equal-arm cross on the Ruby Pillar is removed, the veil of rainbow fire should thin almost to transparency. Then the Three Pillars should be seen to descend into the earth, dissolving as they do so. All the energy of the casting should be grounded. None of the residual energy should be absorbed by any of the participants in its use. The veil of energy that enclosed the triangular shaft of the casting should be reabsorbed by the pillars, but if for any reason it seems to linger it too should be grounded into the earth.

Its Qualities And Uses

Externalized Form
This form of the Three Pillars lends itself well as an adjunct to ritual work such as rising on the planes, shamanic journeys to the Upper or Lower world, and to pathworkings. In addition to making motion between the planes and

---

[2] This is the first layer of energy above the physical.

levels less stressful there is a tendency for the casting to keep a group together as they travel. A byproduct of the method of this casting in the externalized form is the creation of a floor and ceiling that contains the travelers. Although very mundane comparisons— this is in many ways like an elevator, a submarine, or a plane. One of the great benefits of this casting is that it cushions and protects the traveler so that high speed and rapid changes in energy pressure are moderated. There is also a certain amount of protection against intrusion afforded by the veil of Rainbow fire that can be bolstered with other castings and magicks. As a teaching tool, this casting allows teachers to take students to places they cannot yet reliable reach on there own.

The Three Pillars may also be done externally and away from the caster so that they are not within the influence of the casting. In this case the Three Pillars can be used as part of a ritual to charge an object with energy from other planes, spheres, or a particular astrological aspect. To use the Three Pillars in this manner requires keen powers of visualization and refined control of magickal energy. Advanced practitioners may also use this casting in conjunction with evocations using the *triangle of art* [3] or other similar operations to call forth or to summon beings. The clarity and the density of manifestations are greatly increased which can be very good or very bad and definitely not something for the faint of heart. Do not use the Three Pillars for strengthening evocations unless you are an Adept, High Priestess/Priest, or an initiate of some rank.

Internalized Form

One of the best uses for the internalized form is in healing work to channel energy. Of itself the casting does not cause healing energy to flow but it facilitates the use of healing techniques. In rituals where one person becomes the focal point for the energy, the internalized Pillars help to contain and control the flow so that the person may direct the energy with greater finesse. In most cases where discomfort from excess energy is a problem this casting may be useful. There is also a beneficial side-effect in that the dismissal assists in a full grounding at the end of a working. If used regularly as an exercise, this form of the casting can reduce blockages in the subtle bodies.

Microcosmic Form

This is the most mystical form of the Three Pillars in that its primary impact is on the consciousness of the caster. Although you actually create six Pillars in essence they are still three, and this reveals something of the mystery of this casting. This casting lends support to workings or meditations

---

[3] This is a term often applied to a configuration using a triangle within a circle, at whose center is a signal (a symbolic resonator) used to attract and to hold noncorporeal beings. A drogue or a fetish may be substituted for the signal.

that identify the self with the Higher Self or with Deity forms. It does not expand the consciousness rather it creates analogous connections between different orders of consciousness. The microcosmically cast form of the Three Pillars is also useful in workings that involve communicating with entities whose form of consciousness and thought is foreign to the human mode. The expanded set of resonances and correlations of meaning fostered by the Three Pillars helps to bridge the metaphorical *language* barrier.

Principles And Basis For Action

This casting is in part an energy construct and in part a spell relying upon Hermetic principles that describe the resonance between the casting and the underlying structures of reality. The void that lies between the Three Pillars is the void from which all things arise. It is like the negative spaces between the Spheres and the Paths on the Tree that are the lower reflection of the veils of negative existence. It is the ground of being that so resembles a super-saturated solution waiting for the seed of suggestion to burst into form or force. That is the reason that this casting facilitates motion and focus— it is highly sensitive to the action of thought and of intent that is the lower reflection of the primal cause.

The Three Pillars are also a reflection of the primary channels of energy in the human body and subtle bodies. It upholds the natural process of energy flow at the same time that it urges the user to stretch beyond their current limits. It reminds us that we are living proof of the truth of the Microcosm/Macrocosm paradigm.

Limitations And Precautions

Because of the extreme responsiveness of the Three Pillars to the power of thought and intent, it is essential that ritual and mediation be carefully designed with an eye to images and symbols. Those of you that have some experience with pathworkings and with the highways of the mind know that effectiveness or errors often hinge on a single word or theme. This sensitivity with all its potential and hazard is heightened in this casting.

If the externalized form of the casting is used for group ritual it is important to maintain the Veil of Rainbow Fire. Although you may pass through the Veil without disrupting the casting, this action is not without risk. In accordance with the working at hand, there may be a wrenching change in the energy pressure when moving from one side of the Veil to the other. Also, each time the Veil is breached it loses strength that must be replenished.

In the internalized form, if the Three Pillars fail while the practitioner is carrying a large load of energy there is potential for harm. The degree of harm will be in direct relation to the difference between the person's normal capacity and the capacity they are supporting, multiplied by whatever blockages may exist in their subtle bodies at that moment.

I have endeavored to make this book as safe as possible; however the use of the Three Pillars in evocation or manifestation can be dangerous unless handled with expertise. If concentration falters in maintaining the Three Pillars that which is contained with the bounds of the *triangle of art* will be released. This information was included because those who have a bit of creativity or inspiration can stumble across this particular use, and explicit mention and warning was warranted.

Interactions With Other Castings Or Magicks

The Three Pillars are compatible with all the other castings in this book except the Square of Abeyance. However, the strictures against combining other castings still holds true. For example: you can not use the Three Pillars, the Triangle of Stillness, and the Sword and Staff simultaneously. Be mindful of the amount of attention required by the Pillars when designing a ritual that will make use of them, especially if the other components of the ritual will also require active maintenance.

Recommendations For Mastering Its Use

Practice creating, maintaining, and dismissing the Three Pillars as a meditation until it is almost effortless. Then you may use this casting in rituals and workings with confidence and safety. It is possible to cast the Three Pillars with book in hand, but since much of its power depends on the clarity and coherence of the caster the results will be inferior. It is a good idea to have the book in hand while memorizing the steps of the casting. Expanding your knowledge of the Qabala, Chakras, and systems of magick also will have a dramatic effect on the Three Pillars.

More than most castings the Three Pillars in their microcosmic form are a mirror for spiritual development. There is a symbiotic feedback loop between effective use of the microcosmic Three Pillars and progress on a spiritual path. Self-mastery is strengthened by use of this casting as a meditation.

Conclusion

The Three Pillars can be worked into most systems of magick or spiritual development. Do not be put off if you have no interest in the Qabala— the underlying principles that are the foundation for this casting can be found in any Western system. This casting is deceptively simple relative to its potential power, approach it with respect and it will reveal itself.

✒️13✒️

The Star Of Sight

Introduction

The Star of Sight is distinguished from the castings in this book in that it requires a group for its proper functioning. It is also unique in that the casting takes place primarily on the Astral plane with a corresponding echo in the microcosmic Astral of the participants' auras. In some regards it resembles the Three Pillars in that it is an aid to group visioning or group travel, but it encourages a blending of talents. Rather than simply comparing impressions after a group working— the Star of Sight allows for the unification of visions to increase the quality, quantity, and clarity of psychic perceptions. A technique to open the Third Eye that is an integral part of this casting may be used as an individual working. This technique, called the Temple of Isis, must be mastered before the Star of Sight can be used.

The Temple Of Isis

Knowledge of the Chakras is not a prerequisite for the use of this technique, but I urge you to seek out that knowledge because it is so valuable to magickal development. Chakras are the equivalent in the aura of glands and organs in the body and as such are the centers of great activity and are links between the various parts of the self. Although called the Temple of Isis, this method could as easily be called "Temple of the Astral Flame", or "of the Star Goddess". This is not a pantheon-limited technique. Do not attempt the Star of Sight until each member of the working group is comfortable with this technique.

I. The first step is to ground, center, and move into a magickal state of consciousness. Then activate your Third Eye (Brow Chakra) which is located at the center of the forehead. If you do chakra work feel free to use whatever method you normally use to open the chakra and then shape the opened chakra into an oval. If this is new to you begin by creating a spot of brilliant indigo blue energy (the color of new jeans) on your forehead. Expand that point of light until it is a glowing indigo oval like an eye. Feel energy flowing in and out of the Third Eye. Take a deep breath and sing the sound "Ihhh" in a high but comfortable tone near the top of your vocal range. Continue toning until you have raised sufficient energy to make your forehead tingle.

II. Visualize a triangle on the surface of your face connecting the three eyes with a continuous line of energy. The line should begin with the Third Eye and proceed to your right eye, the left, and return to the Third. Ideally the color should also be indigo blue, but you can substitute white or turquoise. Do not use any other colors. When the triangle is stable, fill the triangle with energy. In this case the energy must be indigo to produce the best results.

Move your focus of consciousness to the triangle of energy on the surface of your face. Feel your awareness concentrate itself in that space.

III. Now draw three lines from the vertices of the triangle to its center. The color of these lines should be the same color as the perimeter of the triangle. Then imagine that the lines and the center point are moving back, deep into your brain. See it forming a three sided pyramid whose base remains on the surface of your face. As the flat shape of

Begin

Fill

Forming The Three Sided Pyramid

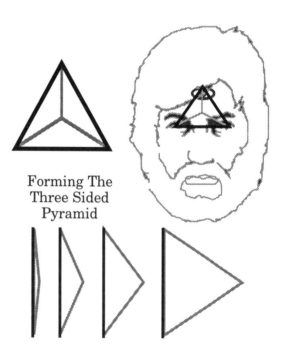

the triangle becomes the three dimensional shape of the pyramid, feel your focus of awareness (consciousness) moving back with it towards the center of your brain. Continue to become more and more focused until your awareness is a point on the tip of the pyramid.

IV. Leaving the energy construct of the pyramid in place, push your awareness through the tip. The vertex of the pyramid is a laya point marking the intersection of different planes of reality. You should pass through an instant of darkness followed by a veil of light. Continue past the veil and find yourself in the Temple of Isis in the pineal gland, deep in your brain. Take a moment to see what is in the Temple. In the center of the floor is a circular hearth containing tall, flickering, blue and violet flames that rise from no visible source. The flames are the Astral fire that is within each of us. The hearth is the seat of that power within us. Take a moment to look at whatever else may be in the chamber. There may be statues, tapestries, altars, or other objects rich in symbolism.

V. Approach the hearth, carefully examine it, and memorize its appearance. You should do this each time you use this technique because the hearth will change. When you are ready step through the flames. You will find that you have moved directly onto the Astral Plane. Proceed with the purpose or working at hand. When you are ready to return look for flames surrounded by the circle (of the hearth) and step through them to the Temple. If you cannot find the flames, call forth the image from your memory and *realize* it.

VI. Reorient yourself to the surroundings of the Temple, making note of any changes. To leave the Temple focus your awareness into a point of brilliance. Move that point of awareness back to the tip of the pyramid. Once again you'll pass through a moment of darkness and a veil of light. Allow your awareness to expand from the point to fill the pyramid. Then flatten the pyramid, changing it back into a triangle on the surface of your face. Allow the triangle to fade and then ground and center thoroughly.

The Star Of Sight

The Calling

This technique is for 5, 7, or 9 people if there is an extra person they may stand or sit in the center during the casting. Do not attempt this casting with fewer than 5 or more than 10. The first step is to scribe a circle with blue or violet fire. You may need to determine the size of the circle prior to its scribing by having the participants lay on the ground. The circle should be large

The Star Of Sight

enough to account for any foot motion people may make while entranced. A 5, 7, or 9 pointed star will also be scribed as a part of this casting. You may wish to take the opportunity when people are on the ground to determine the size of the circle to also place candles to mark the points of the star. You make also wish to use chalk lines or ribbons to outline the star on the ritual ground. The Star should point to the North, the direction of mystery. The candles should be purified and charged specifically for the purpose of the specific working at hand. These candles should be a color appropriate to the working. They should be lit when you are ready to begin.

The participants should stand at their place in the Star as the circle is scribed. Then the Star should be scribed beginning in the North and moving to the South-West in the same manner that an invoking pentacle would be done. If there is an extra person that will be in the center of the Star, they should be the same person that does the scribing. The center is a difficult position and should be reserved for an experienced individual. If the group is an odd number, a blue or violet candle should be placed and lit in the center when the scribing is complete. Then everyone should take their place in the Star configuration and announce their readiness to begin the next step. The scriber should remind the group of the intent of the working, of what information or vision is being sought. All the participants should then open their Transpersonal chakra (or personal Kether). If this is unfamiliar to you then imagine a sphere of brilliant light at the center of the Star, feeling its energy touching the crown of your head. Then the participants should use the Temple of Isis technique. As each person reaches the Astral they should announce their arrival with an "Aum" or some other energy raising vocalization. The Star is complete when all have reached the Astral plane. Seek your vision.

Special Provision

If there is any reason to believe that there will be resistance, opposition, or danger related to the vision or information being sought an additional person will be needed to act as the guardian of the working. The guardian remains outside the circle, armed with a sword, athame, or similar tool of power. They remain vigilant, prepared to banish any unwanted presence that may approach. They also watch for more mundane problems such as cold drafts, household pets, and fires. If for any reason they must cross the boundary of the circle they should say the scriber's name three times and call for an immediate return. They may then cut an opening in the circle and enter it.

The Dismissal

The scriber should use their intuition and insight to determine when either the work has been accomplished or the group is reaching the limit of its endurance. The scriber should summon the hearth and the flame on the Astral and should call for a return with an "Aum" or some other energy raising vocalization. The participants should return from the Temple of Isis and let the sphere of brilliance, their Transpersonal chakra, fade away. After everyone has announced their return, the scriber should put out the candles starting in the center and then progressing through the points of the Star in a banishing pattern. Then all should stand and visualize the violet fire of the Star and Circle dissolving into the Earth. All should ground and center thoroughly. The visions and impressions should be recorded immediately, preferably as food and drink is shared to complete the closing of the psychic centers.

Its Qualities And Uses

The Star of Sight acts as a lens to focus a group's visioning work. It focuses the psychic talents of each of the participants to maximize their effectiveness. It also creates a group mind that has capacities that are the synthesis of the participants' talents with the whole being greater than the sum of the parts. Beyond that, the Star of Sight connects the individual visions and journeys of the participants in a web of synchronicity— of communal meaning. One way to understand the properties of this casting is to consider the difference between a group singing in unison and a chorus.

Principles And Basis For Action

The stars that have 5, 7, or 9 points, when used with magickal intent, open gateways to the other realms. The pentacle is the most commonly used figure for this purpose but its siblings serve just as well. The combination of a star and a circle as used in this casting creates a defined space that holds open the door between the planes. The preferred color of energy falls in the range between blue and violet so as to activate the upper chakras that are most associated with psychism. The number of the participants matches the number of points of the Star and creating a resonant link. The points are identifiable elements of a star and yet are inseparable from the whole. The participants remain themselves but contribute to the formation of a greater whole.

The opening of the Transpersonal chakra (personal Kether) with its placement in the center of the Star performs two functions. In opening the Transpersonal chakra the Higher Self and Higher Will is invoked to help guide the working. The placement of the sphere of brilliance in the center also creates a focal point for the hearth and the flames of the Temple of Isis. The overlapping of the *hearth and the flames* on the inner planes helps to keep the group together as they work. Also the overlap provides a measure of safety for the group. It allows for an easier return because of the clarity of the gateway on the Astral and because it is easily summoned by the scriber.

The flames in the hearth are the Astral fire that is within each of us. This fire is echoed in the flames of the candles. The three fires, the Raith [1] fire of the scribing, the physical fire of the candles, and the Astral fire of the hearth are linked together. The candles also bring with them whatever magick and intent they were charged with prior to the casting. Moreover the physical flames ionize the air, increasing its conductivity, which makes it easier for the participants to connect with each others' energy.

Limitations And Precautions

The greatest limitation is a logical outcome of a casting that is so dependent upon collaboration— everyone must be competent in its use. Do not misunderstand me, everyone need not be a expert nor a diva. This is a *choral* working, the individual voices do not have to be of the first caliber however sour notes are quite noticeable. In those cases where there is an even number of participants resulting in the scriber taking the center position, there is an absolute necessity for that person to be highly skilled. The concentration of energy and pattern in the center is very strong and can be harmful to the person if they are not prepared for the task. Moreover, if the person in the center is overwhelmed by the power, the casting will be disrupted as they fall out

---

[1]   Magickal energy shaped by an incarnate soul.

of concert with the rest of the participants.

Of itself, the Star of Sight does not provide much protection against intrusion by unwanted influences and presences. The scribing of the circle will stop some things but it is hardly the bulwark of a Quarters-cast circle. Most of the defense is in the power of the group mind created by the casting. In most cases the strength of the group mind is a sufficient deterrent to interference. In those cases where it is not, then the role of the guardian becomes essential. Be sure that you are clear on any risks associated with the information you seek.

It is very important that everyone be grounded, centered, and their psychic senses sealed at the end of any ritual using this casting. The expansion of the senses and the involvement of the Higher Self in the creation of a short-lived but powerful group mind can produce prolonged side-effects if a person does not attend to the important task of returning to a normal state of being. One of the possible side-effects is damage to the coherence of the *magickal personality*.

Warning: Do not attempt to use this casting to access the information stored in the Akashic Records . There is a heavy and unpredictable price for doing so as an individual and it is multiplied by this casting. There are many planes, time frames, and places where information can be safely gathered. Many people confuse the information that they gather on the other planes with accessing the Akashic Records. The Akashic Records are like the mind of the Ultimate Source of the Universe, and are an inner sanctum that can only be touched with impunity if that touch is by the invitation of the Great Ones.

Interactions With Other Castings Or Magicks

There are only two castings that are compatible with the Star of Sight, those being the Triangle of Stillness and the Quarters-cast circle. The Triangle as well as the Quarters-cast circle must be cast large enough to completely enclose the scribed circle of the Star. Combining a Triangle *and* a Quarters-cast circle with the Star is not advisable for reasons that should become apparent. The Triangle can greatly assist in the creation of a space where the integration of the individual talents with the group mind is enhanced, but the Triangle weakens the strength of the scribed boundary on the other planes. The attenuated boundary means that the Star's already marginal protective qualities are made virtually nil. The Quarters-cast circle does create a strong defensive boundary, but it tends to act as an anchor which limits mobility on the other planes. If the Triangle and Quarters-cast circle are used together in this context they tend to cancel out each other's benefits.

Generally speaking, whatever rituals are used in the preparation of the candles will be compatible with the Star of Sight. The same is true for any incense that you may use as well.

Recommendations For Mastering Its Use

Full command of the Temple of Isis technique is the single most important factor in using the Star. You may wish to tape the instructions for the Temple of Isis or have a friend read them to you until you have memorized the protocol. You may also have the scriber guide the group through the technique during the casting of the Star. Having one person lead the group in this casting is infinitely better than having everyone trying to read the one page summary of the Star while the casting is underway.

Once you and your working group have familiarized yourselves with the Star of Sight you can begin to modify it to your particular style or tradition. These modifications should be limited to the way that you open the Transpersonal chakra and the addition of invocations to the Deities. Asking for the support and the counsel of the Great Ones in the seeking of visions is always a prudent choice. I cannot guess at the impact of any changes to the protocol of the Star beyond those two. I do not recommend experimentation unless you are an old hand at magick and have a deep understanding of this casting.

Conclusion

The Star of Sight is presented late in this book because it is definitely not for beginners. It is a very potent tool for finding answers, for rediscovering what has been lost, or for bringing new information into the here and now. You may find the Temple of Isis technique apropos to other ritual patterns that you use or as a working in itself. Of all the castings in this book, it is the one that most resembles a spell in its internal structure. Like a spell, the Star of Sight is very much a product of the skill and the intent of the casters. Do not underestimate the power of a seemingly simple casting such as the Star.

14

The Four Minds

This chapter describes the Four Minds ritual for divination. This is not a casting but it is a ritual whose use helps to sharpen the skills that are used in castings. Another benefit arising from the application of the Four Minds ritual is a deeper understanding of the Elements and their realms. I have found that the Four Elements are also Four Minds, four distinct ways of grappling with the perception and the understanding of experiences. Some refer to these ways of knowing as "The Four Powers Of The Sphinx": Earth- the power to be silent; Air- the power to know; Fire- the power to will; Water- the power to dare. The concept of the Four Powers is an excellent starting point in understanding the Four Minds. In my tradition, as has been mentioned earlier, the Four Elements plus Ether are most generally thought of as corresponding to the Five Holy Parts of Self, (Air- Mind, Fire- Soul, Water- Heart, Earth- Body, Ether- Spirit).

In addition to these correlations to the Self, the Elements are also thought of as being intertwined throughout every part of our being because on this level of reality no pure elemental forms exist. We are all a mixture of the Elements of creation, and in turn each part of us is some blending of the Elements, the interplay of blendings reflecting the macrocosm and the microcosm in an infinitely recursive pattern. But, to understand the blendings it is necessary to know of the pure forms in the same way that an artist must know the primary colors and the outcomes of their combinations. The Four Minds ritual is an exercise in experiencing the primary Elemental colors and their blendings.

A natural outgrowth of my experimentation with the Four Elements as Four Minds led to the realization that they provide a useful pattern and rhythm for divination and meditation. One of the great difficulties in divination or meditation for a specific purpose is the fine balance that must be sought between active and passive modes of thought and perception. One must be open to receive visions, but focused for a purpose to tune in to a specific vision. One must be nonresistant to receive guidance, but guarded against unwanted intrusion or manipulation. One must be open to the flow of the higher language of intuition and psychism, but editing to understand

119

or to translate the message into the intelligible expressions of daily life. Additionally, the need to stay clear, or at least cognizant of the hopes, fears, and desires that might sway or distort insights is imperative.

The Elements as the Four Minds give structure and stability to the question of balance and harmony in divination and visioning by providing an external reference that is internally meaningful. The Elements in the form of the Four Minds each have specific modes of sensation, perception, and thought that are natural and self-reinforcing. The Elements also have relationships to each other that exist in the frames of time, space, and meaning. The connections between the internal and external realities and frames of reference promote the development of bridges of meaning. Taking what I know of the Four Minds, I have developed an inner ritual that articulates the various steps needed for successful psychic divination or meditation on a specific question. I call this a ritual rather than a technique because it is a cycle of actions forming an organic whole. The Four Minds can be folded into other rituals or expanded upon, but it must retain its basic pattern to be effective.

The Tattvas

The symbols and colors used in this ritual are a common variant of the Tattvas as used by the Golden Dawn and should be familiar to those with Ceremonial magick. For many Neo-Pagans the symbols do not make immediate poetic sense as icons for the Elements. Likewise, the color scheme of the Tattvas does not match the color schemes commonly used by Neo-Pagans. I have found the Tattvas to be very useful and have intuited visual associations that ground them in the bardic sensibility of Neo-Paganism. Air is represented by a blue circle that depicts the blue dome of the sky, like air that surrounds us. Fire is represented by a red triangle that is a stylized flame, sharp edged with the bite of fire. Water is represented by a silver crescent that reminds us that water has no color, holds light, and is ruled by the Moon. Earth is represented by a yellow square, yellow for gold the highest vibration of matter and the rectilinear solidity of a square with the echo of the four quarters in its form. Spirit is represented by an egg that may be black, clear, or all colors that stands for the infinite possibilities of creation within the parameters of its order.

Preparation

Take as much time as you need to formulate your question or meditation topic. When the words, images, and feelings associated with your question are solidly in your grasp you may begin. Ground and center using your preferred method, making certain that you set aside extraneous concerns as much as is possible. Then at the center point of your being, the core of your consciousness, place the image of an egg. The egg may be clear, like quartz crystal, black like obsidian, or flashing with many colors like an opal. When engaged in this ritual you may return to the egg of Spirit/ Ether in your center whenever you need to rebalance or to refocus. After visualizing the egg, imagine that you are on a flat. featureless plain standing next to the egg.

Earth (1)

Yellow

Water (4) Silver

Clear Black All

Ether (Ø)

Blue

Air (2)

Red

Fire (3)

Earth: Step 1

In your inner landscape look to the North. Allow your instincts to tell you where North is in this inner realm. Visualize a yellow square glowing in the North. Take a breath then imagine passing through it like a portal to the realm of the Mind of Earth. Look around and attend to what you see. Then remain passive, silent and open to all impressions, especially bodily or internal sensations. Clear your mind, and remember that Earth is the essence of form and pattern. When you feel prompted to move on, return through the portal of the yellow square to the plain.

Air: Step 2

In your inner landscape look to the East. The direction for East in this inner realm should be 90° clockwise from wherever you determined North to be. Visualize a blue circle glowing in the East, then imagine passing through it like a portal into the Mind of Air. Look around and attend to what you see. Then try to understand what you sensed in the Mind of Earth. The clouds, winds, and dust about you take the form of your thoughts. Try to brainstorm different meanings and interpretations. See if new pieces of information or insight arise in the flux. When you feel prompted to move on, return through the portal of the blue circle to the plain.

Fire: Step 3

In your inner landscape look to the South, place it directly opposite the North. Visualize a red triangle glowing in the South, then imagine passing through it like a portal into the Mind of Fire. Look around and attend to what you see. Summon your desire for the knowledge or insight that you are seeking. Fan the flames of will so that you may have the strength to seek the truth. Concentrate on your determination to will power then return through the portal of the red triangle.

Water: Step 4

In your inner landscape look to the West. Visualize a silver crescent shining in the West, then imagine passing through it like a portal into the Mind of Water. Look around and attend to what you see. Summon your courage, your heart, and open to whatever may come. Allow all the emotions related to the question to wash over you and flow through you. Take note of the meanings, the flavors, and the nuances that the sentiments bring. Return through the portal of the silver crescent to the plain and go to egg.

Ether: Step 5 (Ø)

Standing at the center of the plain in your inner landscape, place the egg once more in the center point of your being. Transmit to the egg all information, all the understanding, and all the answers that you gained in the Four Minds. You may speak to the egg, write on it, or use whatever other metaphor for communication seems appropriate. Tell yourself that everything that you need to remember will be remembered, know that it is so. After communing with the egg, listen to see if it has any message for you.

—Repeat The Cycle—

Start again with the yellow square of Earth and repeat the full cycle. Do not end in the middle of a cycle. Continue until you have gathered the information or insight that you were seeking or you are tired and are no longer able to focus. With each cycle there will be greater resolution, clarity, and depth of perception. Generally, it takes at least three cycles for good results.

Closure

At the end of a cycle, return to the egg in your center point. Recreate the state of being grounded and centered. Listen to your body and take an energy inventory, watching for any changes that may be messages related to the question or topic that you were investigating. When you feel solid place any critical pieces of information/insight into the egg. Take a few deep breaths, open your eyes, and begin to move slowly to fully return from the inner landscape. As soon as you are able, make a written log of the session. If you dread writing use a tape recorder to capture any fleeting impressions. In the hours or days after the ritual if you forget something or need clarification, close your eyes and return briefly to the egg. Additionally, pay close attention to any dreams that you recall from the night after the ritual.

Recommendations

Although most people have a good experience the first time that they perform this ritual, there is a sizable improvement in its efficacy as the symbols and the ritual becomes more familiar. It also takes some time to develop stamina to complete a series of cycles through the Four Minds. Persistence does pay , in this case the rewards are generous. You may wish to create a diagram of a circle with the five shapes in their appropriate colors as a visual aid. Another alternative, if you would prefer to keep your eyes shut, is a cord tied in a circle with the shapes (cut from cardboard, etc.) hung from the cord like charms in their sequence. The shapes may be fingered as a prompt to help remember your place in the cycle. Creating these or other aids is also a way to speed the memorization of this ritual. I have found this to be a simple but powerful ritual. Feel free to adapt it to your needs and belief system. Good luck and clear sight.

◘ Some general thoughts on divination are presented on page 124 for you to consider after using the Four Minds.

Thoughts On Divination

Divined Information comes from
three primary sources:

**Sources Of
Information**

Intelligences

This can be the individual consciousness of
any being or the collective consciousness of
any group. The intelligence contacted may be
of any of the levels of consciousness possible or
a combination of those levels. This runs the full
spectrum of consciousness up to the Divine.

Imprints & Artifacts

All thoughts and actions leave a mark on the
subtle weave of reality. The imprints and artifacts
of events may be read regardless of their location in space and time
because their pattern is recorded in eternity (outside of linear time).

Observations

Consciousness may travel through space and time and observe events.
Also the powers of the mind to find pattern and create meaning from
fragmentary clues should not be underestimated.

The Two Greatest Sources Of Interference

Attachment: Attachment breeds fear of knowledge and
false sensings.

Translation: Lack of metaphorical vocabulary leads to
loss of detail and literalism.

Divinatory techniques are generally a
combination of three broad approaches:

Tools & Systems
Psychic Methods
Magick & Ritual

The proportion of the combinations varies
with the methods and the individuals
using the methods.

☀15☀

The Circle Of Sound

Introduction

The power of the human voice when used without words to make tones is a greatly under-rated tool in the creation of sacred space. When we make sounds without words we reach deeply into the soul. Chants that use words can be very powerful, but pure sound helps to minimize the impact of the ego-self. When we make tones we do so not only with our physical bodies but with our subtle bodies as well. The physical vibrations that we call sound are the anchor for subtle vibrations that move energy and alter consciousness on several levels. The Circle Of Sound is a compelling and elegantly simple casting that can be used to augment other ritual forms or as a free-standing working in its own right. This casting uses no tools other than the human voice and intent.

Before describing the casting itself, I'd like to make a distinction between singing and chanting. Many people are skeptical about their capacity to sing since society makes value judgments about *good* and *bad* voices. Certainly singing is an art form with all the standards applicable to art, but chanting is a craft. I have been in a number of rituals where some of the best chanting came from the poorest singing voices. Chanting is about raising energy and consciousness with clear intention, often backed by strong emotion. Think about the word *enchant* (in chant) and its other forms: enchantment, enchanted, enchantress then meditate on the roots of magick in sound. Think also on the word *incantation* that when taken to its Latin roots means *in song* (cantus).

The casting of the Circle of Sound creates a space that encourages: the formation of a group mind, ease in the pooling of energies, and emotional comfort. The sense of being in a space apart from the rest of the world is very strong, but unlike other castings it feels more like being in a valley or a hollow rather than behind walls. Empathy and telepathy between those enclosed in a Circle of Sound is fostered by this casting. Although it can be done as a solo working, the Circle of Sound works best with 3 to 35 participants.

To prepare for the Circle of Sound casting you should prepare your voice. Chanting requires physical exertion and should be treated like any other physical activity. I am certain that you have been told that it is important for an athlete to stretch their muscles and tendons before engaging in their sport. Warming up exercises help to increase performance and reduce the likelihood of injury. Warming up your voice is important. You may wish to make the following exercises part of your preparations for this and other workings that use the voice.

Exercises

1) Breathing: Take slow breaths and begin to pay attention to how your body feels as the air moves in and out. Take progressively deeper breaths to explore and expand your current lung capacity. Don't be afraid to stick out your belly when you inhale deeply; the deepest breathing comes from the belly not the chest. After reacquainting yourself with your breathing and body begin the process of warming up your voice by taking deep breaths, letting the air out slowly making a quiet hissing sound. This builds breath control which is essential to chanting.

2) Humming: After finishing with the quiet hissing, begin to hum a low deep tone that you can feel vibrating in your chest. Continue humming the low tone until you feel your throat relax. Slowly change the deep low hum to a higher tone. You should feel the vibration move upwards from your chest toward your head. Hum from a low tone to a high tone several times until you can track the movement of the vibration in your body.

3) Toning: Take a deep breath and chant: "Ahh-Ooo-Omm" letting the closing "m" vibrate upon your lips. Don't try for volume, instead try for a smooth transition between each set of sounds. As you form this sound listen carefully and continue listening into the silence following the closing "m". This extended version of the Aum moves the mouth, tongue, and breath through all the positions required to finish preparing the voice.

The Calling

Prior to beginning this casting all who are participating should prepare their voices using the exercises offered in this chapter. Then the group should form a circle and join hands. While holding hands, everyone grounds and centers using the tree exercise presented in chapter 5. Make sure that there is imagery that encourages the intertwining of the roots and branches of all who are in the circle. Close this part of the casting with the image of the people having become a sacred grove and drop hands. Whoever is acting as the primary caster should raise energy by toning "Aum" once. As the "mmm" is still vibrating on their lips they should take the hand of the person to their left and pass the energy that has been raised to them. Then that person should make an Aum and then take the hand of the person to their left and pass the energy. As the process repeats itself the energy of the group is harmonized. When it comes back around to the primary caster the first part of the casting is complete. The primary caster should send some energy clockwise through the linked hands to affirm this step. Then he or she should bring together the hands of the people to their right and left so that they may step out of the circle of hands.

At that point any other casters, and ideally there should be 1-3 more, will execute the same maneuver so that they can step out of the circle. The other casters should move clockwise around the perimeter of the circle until they reach the primary caster. The casters face outward away from the circle and join hands. They begin to make tones together which can be any combination of vowel sounds or Aum. As a group, while holding hands, they move clockwise around the perimeter of the circle. The casters who are furthest to the left and right will each have a free hand that should be raised to direct the energy in the scribing of the circle. The sound should be as continuous as possible. The casters should monitor each others breathing so that they do not all pause in their chanting at the same time. When they make one complete circuit they join hands with those that are in the circle. The entire group then raises one Aum together. The casting of the Circle of Sound is complete at this point.

The Dismissal

To dismiss the Circle of Sound the group sits or kneels on the ground. Each person is asked to listen with their inner ear for the sound that describes the essence of the place and the moment. This can be any sound. Then in unison, the group makes whatever sound that springs from within, directing the sound and the energy earthwards. Everyone should ground and center.

Its Qualities And Uses

Group Building: This casting may be used to prepare a space for a group to engage in important discussions, consensus building, or conflict resolution. It can also be an adjunct to workings to build or make contact with a group mind or egregore [1]. Rituals to seek the sponsorship and support of discarnate beings for collective work may be strengthened with the addition of this casting.

---

[1] A term that in this case is the group mind of a Tradition or a magickal group of long standing.

Healing Rituals: Because this casting helps to harmonize the energy of all the participants, the sharing of energy in healing is encouraged. In many ways the actions of the casting help to bring everyone into the same energy key. Moreover, people get in touch with their capacity to move and channel energy through the Circle of Sound so are more prepared to engage in healing work.

Work With Nature: The Circle of Sound is an act of beauty and harmony that can be sensed on many planes of reality. This casting is not a fortress; it is more like a bower or sacred enclosure. Nature spirits, devas, and the faerie folk see it as a welcoming space that does not wall them out. The emotional tone of the participants in a Circle of Sound is generally softened and sweetened which also makes contact with the powers of nature more likely.

Meditation: This casting encourages serenity and sharpness of perception and hence is a great aid to meditative or contemplative work. The simplicity of the casting makes it attractive for group meditation. Since no special equipment is needed and it takes little time to set up or take down, the Circle of Sound could fit into the process of a weekly meditation group easily. Confidence Building: For novices this is a great confidence builder because almost everyone has an immediate and recognizable experience of magick in this casting. It also encourages people to use their voice as a tool for raising energy and consciousness. It is especially good for those people who find it hard to see energy.

Principles And Basis For Action

One of the great Hermetic principles is that all is vibration. In most magick the primary sensory modality is sight and the metaphor for energy becomes light in all its colors. Light is vibration and sound is vibration and so the two are metaphorically one. In this casting we use sound vibrations to create an energy structure and in the process of so doing the energy of the group coalesces. The Circle of Sound is created by the sound coming *from* the people and by that sound being *heard* by the people. In hearing the sounds, the reality of the energy structure becomes multi-dimensional in the minds of the participants. Another of the Hermetic principles is that all is mind. The sounds that are heard by the physical ears combine with the sounds heard by the inner ear to create a current that carries the participants to another level of being [2].

---

[2]   There are three Sanskrit words that were the source of my insight this process. Ahata are sounds that we hear with our ears. Anahata are the subtle sounds of energy. Shabda is river of sounds that can carry us beyond the physical.

Limitations And Precautions

This is a simple and gentle working and so long as you keep that in mind harm is unlikely. The Circle of Sound has some protective qualities since positive energy calls to positive energy, but this casting does not create a bulwark against intrusion by negative forces. It may also have the somewhat desirable side-effect of speeding the awakening of the psychic centers which depending upon the person or situation can be a mixed blessing. It is also not uncommon for people to feel that it is unnecessary to ground after this casting because the energy flow is so smooth— this is a mistake.

Interactions With Other Castings Or Magicks

It can be combined with the other castings in this book with the exception of the Square of Abeyance. It works particularly well with a Quarters-Cast circle and not so well with the Triangle of Stillness. Because the energy of the Circle of Sound is married to the place and time where it is created, the local energy atmosphere and the prevailing astrological conditions will have a significant influence. If the energy or the acoustics of a place are not suitable the quality of the casting will suffer accordingly.

Recommendations For Mastering Its Use

Regular use of the warm up exercises is essential to mastering of this casting. Becoming comfortable and happy with the sound of your own voice is equally important. If you cringe at the sound of your own voice on a recording, you have a lot of work to do. Think of your voice as an extension of your

Brainwaves, Frequencies, & Elements

Wave	Freq.	Qualities	Element
Beta	14-20 hz	Alert Cognition, Waking Consciousness	Air
Alpha	8-13 hz	Visualization, Daydream, Meditation	Fire
Theta	4-7 hz	Dream, Shamanism, Visions	Water
Delta	.5 - 3 hz	Deep Sleep, Profound Trance	Earth

soul and honor it. Remember to strive for quality and control— not volume. The loudness of your chanting does not correlate directly to the amount of energy raised. However, if you and your fellows are all whispering or mouthing without making sounds, not much will happen.

If you would like to experiment with rhythms and magick, the information in figure 1 should give you some food for thought.

Conclusions

I strongly recommend this casting for magickal working groups and study groups. It takes little time to achieve proficiency and the results of its regular use are significant. The Circle of Sound is an easy way to add one more elements to focus to the energy in rituals.

❧16❧

Planning For Large Rituals

Introduction

Sooner or later most groups are tempted or encouraged to host a ritual for a large number of people. These larger rituals can prove very valuable in fostering community and in building ties of understanding. Larger rituals can also be terrible disappointments or embarrassments. Even if the individuals or groups involved are accomplished and confident ritualists within the scale of their small group setting, the critical requirements of larger rituals may elude them. This chapter offers some suggestions for making success a higher probability. An entire book could (and may be) written on this topic, but hopefully these will be a useful starting point. I will use the example of a specific ritual in order to ground the suggestions in concrete detail.

In June of 1992, Keepers of the Holly Chalice coordinated a successful main ritual, called "Calling Forth The Faery Child", at the Free Spirit Alliance's gathering in Maryland. Despite a record number of attendees at the main ritual (around 300), far above what was anticipated, the ritual achieved its goals. As with every ritual, planning involved much discussion about the proper use of color, symbols, themes, chants, etc, but the planning group was especially concerned with the particular problems created by size and scale. These were some of the problems that were identified:

Initial Considerations

- Making a clear transition from Gathering/Social headspace to Ritual headspace.
- No way to know how many people will attend the ritual, and the need to plan accordingly.
- People tend to be far away from each other resulting in difficulty in seeing each other, hearing each other, and feeling the group energy.
- Difficulty in coordinating chants or motion.
- Making space/accommodations for people unable to stand through a long ritual or small children.
- Is the site safe? How likely is interruption or interference?

The following were some of the solutions applied to the challenges of a large group ritual. When implemented, they were far from perfect, but they did make a significant difference. More importantly, they were able to accommodate last minute changes at the ritual. With modification they could be used in many types of rituals.

The Faerie Gate

We set up three arches made of bent saplings adorned with ribbons and boughs of oak, ash, and thorn. Four people, two with sage smudge sticks, and two with salt water and tree branch aspergers, stood to either side of the Gate and chanted as people passed through. Having a tangible representation of a gate and the sound of chanting helped people to make a mental transition into ritual. This arrangement gave us a lot of control over the rate at

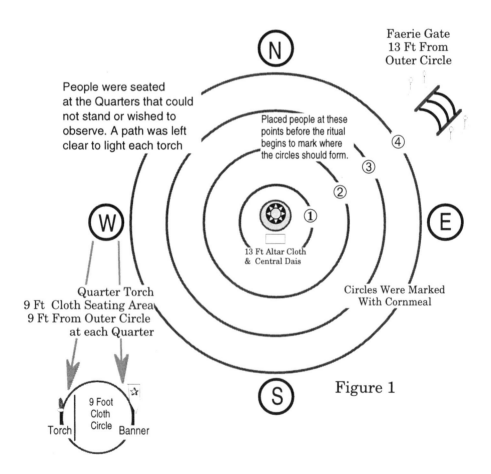

Faerie Gate
13 Ft From
Outer Circle

People were seated at the Quarters that could not stand or wished to observe. A path was left clear to light each torch

Placed people at these points before the ritual begins to mark where the circles should form.

13 Ft Altar Cloth & Central Dais

Quarter Torch
9 Ft Cloth Seating Area
9 Ft From Outer Circle
at each Quarter

Circles Were Marked With Cornmeal

9 Foot Cloth Circle

Torch   Banner

Figure 1

which people entered the circle which was critical to the next step. Having an identified Gate also made it easier for people to leave the ritual in an orderly manner while it was being conducted. In large semi-public rituals it is not unusual to have individuals needing to leave before a ritual is completed. (See Figure 1)

Concentric Circles

We had decided to place people in 4 concentric circles, so that people would be closer to each other. Given that we could not know how many people would be attending the ritual we had to devise a system that was self-adjusting. After many considerations we settled on a simple counting method. A person stood just past the Faerie Gate, inside the circle, and counted off 4 people and sent them to the outermost circle, counted off 3 people and sent them to the next one in, then 2 people to the inner circle, and 1 person to the innermost. Some helpers ushered people to their appropriate circle while others stood at appropriate distances from the center of the ritual ground as markers for the circles to form. The day of the ritual we made our best guess on how many would be attending and used basic geometry to set up the ritual ground. We marked the ground with cornmeal as a guide to maintaining the geometry of the circles. Cornmeal was chosen because it also acted as a gift to the spirits of the land.

Puck & The Hideous Pink Headbands

To address the problem of coordinating chanting and group movement we had one of our members act as Puck, our master of ceremonies and official trickster. He was free to move from circle to circle with words of encouragement, admonishment, and a strong singing voice. Additionally, there were about 35 people wearing highly visible fluorescent pink headbands distributed throughout the circles that knew the chants and the ritual. We'd made an announcement during the morning meeting at the gathering to follow the lead of those wearing the headbands.

Ask For Help

Large groups are easier to manage and flow smoothly if you have enough people that can take an active part in leading and facilitating the ritual. A good rule of thumb might be 1 person who knows the ritual for every 15 in attendance. Keepers of the Holly Chalice did not have 35 people in their group, and most groups putting on large open rituals don't either. Keepers asked for help. Their sister coven, Coven of the Sacred Drum, and friends at the gathering provided the additional people power that was needed. They were kind enough to consent to the wearing of the hideous pink headbands. They also helped with the onerous task of moving all the props and decorations to the site which reduced last minute hurry and nerves.

Let People Know What To Expect

An enlarged and laminated outline of "Calling Forth The Faery Child" was posted at the main kiosk and bulletin board for the gathering. Copies of the ritual outline were also available at the registration desk. A practice session was held over lunch the day of the ritual to go over the outline and to practice chants. Letting people know what to expect at a ritual helps the ritual go smoothly. It also allows people to make an informed choice as to whether they wish to attend the ritual. Don't worry about losing the element of surprise in the ritual. The element of surprise is often present whether or not it is invoked.

Five To Call The Quarters

To make it easier to hear the calls to the Quarters and to encourage active group participation in the magick we had five people reciting the invocations in unison. The five moved from Quarter to Quarter like the hands of a clock. Four were a step beyond each of the concentric circles, and one was at the outermost, scribed, perimeter of the ritual ground bearing a huge two-handed sword. In addition to the considerations of audibility and visibility in a large ritual, it takes considerably more energy to delineate a large circle. A group casting often works more effectively in these cases. (See Figure 2).

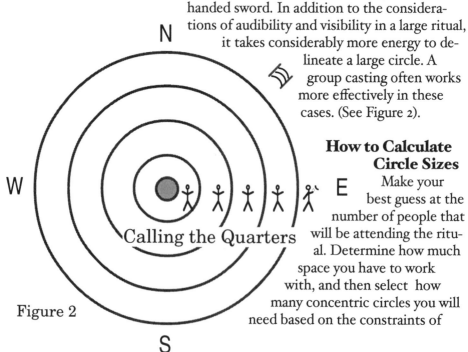

Calling the Quarters

Figure 2

How to Calculate Circle Sizes

Make your best guess at the number of people that will be attending the ritual. Determine how much space you have to work with, and then select how many concentric circles you will need based on the constraints of numbers, space, and ritual format. I found it useful to construct a table of values to check as needed. Remember not to confuse diameter with radius in the set-up.

The spread from hand-to-hand is a generous 4 ft to allow for extensive group movement. If you calculate using 3 ft you can fit more people into a smaller space and in most rituals this is enough. For example- 100 people will fit in a 95 ft diameter circle instead of a 127 ft circle using 3 ft per person. I've calculated 2 tables as an example in figure 3. As you can see, you may focus on the number of people expected and/or the space available in making your determinations.

Three Concentric Circles

Extensive Motion (4 feet Spread)		Normal Motion (3 feet Spread)	
Total Number of People= 60		Total Number of People= 84	
Space Available ≈ 40 feet		Space Available ≈ 40 feet	
Subtotal	Diameter	Subtotal	Diameter
30	38 feet	42	40 feet
20	25 feet	28	28 feet
10	12.5 feet	14	13 feet
Span Between Circles ≈ 6.5 feet		Span Between Circles ≈ 7 feet	
Total Number of People= 90		Total Number of People= 120	
Space Available ≈ 60 feet		Space Available ≈ 60 feet	
Subtotal	Diameter	Subtotal	Diameter
45	57 feet	60	57 feet
30	38 feet	40	38 feet
15	19 feet	20	19 feet
Span Between Circles ≈ 9.5 feet		Span Between Circles ≈ 9.5 feet	

Figure 3

The Math

Diameter= Circumference/π

Circumference= Diameter x π

$\pi \approx 3.14159$ ¤ Hand to hand spread = 4 feet (or 3 feet)

Circumference= Number of People x Hand Spread

Span Between Circles= (Diameter - Diameter)/2

Safety & Privacy

Since this event took place at a campground during a gathering there was little chance of interruption by outsiders. This is an important issue in some circumstances, and requires the posting of watchers to guard the ritual space. This ritual involved a fair amount of motion so the original site selected by the festival organizers was unacceptable because there was a significant slope to the ground. Despite moving the ritual to more level ground, there was still a twisted ankle and a hurt back as a result of post ritual dancing. One blind spot in the plans for this ritual was the need to attend to the crowd *after* the ritual was over. Provisions had been made to help people ground and center after the ritual, but helping people move out of the ritual ground was not a consideration.

Knowing Your Part

In the closeness and intimacy of a small ritual a glance or a nod across the room can be enough of a cue to ensure the smooth flow of a ritual. Those same subtle signals generally don't work in a large ritual. There is no substitute for actually knowing the order of the ritual and your part in it. Hosting a large ritual will also reveal how much a group relies on the memory of one or two members, rather than sharing responsibility. In addition to creating and distributing an outline of the ritual for the attendees, it is helpful to have a script that allow the people putting on the ritual to study their part in detail. Pages 137 & 138 of this chapter offer examples from the Faery Child ritual.

Think Big, Think Small

In designing a ritual for a large group consider the difference that scale makes. How long will each step or section of the ritual take? Will the decorations be visible? If the incense is important, have you made enough to smolder in the large quantities needed to affect a large volume of air. Whenever possible, actually test your ideas. Do not rely upon thought experiments. Take out the 50 foot tape measure and see if things actually sound or look the way you anticipated. A critical part of our ritual involved a symbolic Great Rite[1]. Had this occurred at ground level it would not have been visible so we created a raised platform using a table top, crates, and cloth. We tested the platform before the ritual. I believe that much of the beauty and the focus of a small group ritual can be captured in large groups if the differences and the similarities of the big and the small are considered.

---

[1] The Great Rite is a union of a blade and a cup as a symbolic representation of sexual union. It is rare for the Great Rite to be enacted as actual sexual intercourse.

— Excerpt From The Script For The Ritual —

Ritual Ground Set-Up [b]

1b)   Measure & Mark Circles
Use a stake, cord, and cornmeal to lightly scribe the 4 circles on the ritual ground.

2b)   Quarters
Place torches, cloth circles, and banners at the Quarters.

3b)   Altar
Place altar cloth on ground. Set up dais. Arrange decorations.

4b)   Faerie Gate
Set up the three gates. Hang Oak, Ash, Thorn boughs and sigils.

Procession [c]

1c)   The Drums Call
Tell the drummers to start, slowly at first.

2c)   Puck Leads Us
Puck leads us in silent procession around the camp leading to the Ritual Ground. Puck's helpers ring chimes and bells.

3c)   Lady & Lord
The Lady & The Lord are in the center moving into aspect as the procession approaches the ritual ground. They sit quietly on thrones.

Roles & Props

1b)   Stake with swivel. Pre-measured cord. 3 large   corn meal containers from BJs. (Ivo)

2b)   4 Tiki torches. 4 cloth circles, 4 banners. (various)

3b)   Altar cloth, dais [milk crates, door, cloth], cauldron, cup & athame, flowers, and other decorations.   Candles in jars.(various)

4b)   Gate, sigils, boughs, candles in jars. (Seelie Court)

————————◇————————

2c) Nancy, Janice, etc to bring chimes
3c)   2 chairs draped with cloth

Puck— Jim Scroggs

Lady & Lord— Helena & Michael

Notes:

Note:

Each person who had any part in the ritual had a 5 page script that they could work with prior to the ritual. This script was also used as a checklist before the ritual to ensure that all the preparations had been made.

Calling Forth The Faery Child

FSA ◊ 6/20/92 ◊ Summer Solstice ◊ Moon In Pisces

Ritual Outline

Puck is our master of ceremonies; heed him and his helpers this night. The magic of the Drums calls you to the Ritual Ground.

I. Purification At The Faerie Gate

Pass beneath the Three Gates hung with boughs of Oak, Ash, & Thorn. Listen to the Avallach chant at the Gate, and let it carry you— but don't join in the chant. This chant opens the Faerie Gate. Smell the sage and sense the power of fire and air. Feel the salt water and sense the power of earth and water.

II. Casting The Circle

Upon entering the ritual ground you will be assigned to one of 4 concentric circles. If you have difficulty with movement or have small children you may wish to sit at the Quarters. The Circle is scribed and when the last torch in the North is lit the drumming stops. **No one may enter the ritual ground after the drums stop**.

Listen and lend your energy as the Quarters are called.

After the Quarters are called, the outermost circle begins to move clockwise and and chants: "Circle Is Cast" [Chant ①]. Then at the end of the first verse the next circle inwards begins to move and chant. This pattern repeats until all 4 circles are moving clockwise and singing "Circle Is Cast" as a round. As the energy peaks the outer circle will stop moving and sings only the last line of the chant: "A circle is cast! A circle is cast!" The other circles stop moving, in sequence, and we end in unison with: "A circle is cast! A circle is cast!"

Note: If you are at one of the Quarters, chant with the outer circle.

III. Statement Of Intent

Listen to the Lady and the Lord of Faerie as they shape and frame the intent of this ritual to call forth the younger self and create a faery child of the Sun.

IV. Invoking The Ocean Womb

As the banners at the Quarters are brought to the center of the ritual ground we sing "Mother Carry Me" [chant ②] and sway in place. Visualize waves of ocean power moving to the center of the circle.

V. Great Rite & Cauldron of Rebirth

The Lady and the Lord of Faerie bid us to assist them in the creation of the faery child. They enact a symbolic Great Rite then pour the waters of their union into the Cauldron of Rebirth.

VI. Invoking The Faery Sun

When the Lady and the Lord begin to focus energy on the Cauldron we sing: "Infinite Sun" [Chant ③]. Visualize joining the power of the Sun with the Ocean to form a child of light.

VII. Welcoming The Faery Child

When the Lady and the Lord raise their arms and proclaim the birth of the child, the chanting stops. The drumming begins again and all are encouraged to welcome the spirit of the child with dancing and merry-making.

VIII. The Circle Is Open

Remain and dance as long as you like. When you wish to depart do so through the Gate. Before leaving take a stone marked with the glyph of the Sun from the Cauldron of Rebirth as a blessing and reminder. The circle will be dismissed late in the night when the celebrants tire.

Merry Meet, Merry Part, And Merry Meet Again!

∽ Chants ∽

"Avallach, Tir Nan Og, Annwn!"

(ahv-Alhl-ach, Teer-nahn-Auk, Ah-Noon)
{Avalon, The Land of Youth, The Underworld}
Note: Listen for this chant at the Gate, and let it carry you but don't join in the chant.

①

"A circle is cast.
Again, and again, and again and
A circle is cast..."

②

"The River she is flowing,
flowing and growing.
The River she is flowing, down to the sea.
Mother carry me your child I will always be.
Mother carry me, down to the sea."

③

"We are one with the infinite Sun,
forever, and ever, and ever."

{If you know the Native American words
to this chant sing them.}

17

Closing Thoughts

Through this book you have encountered a diverse collection of castings that I hope you will master and use responsibly. Like so many others who have offered how-to help, I shall not hold myself responsible if you don't wear your safety glasses or if you take the guard off the blade. With that final caveat given, I'd like to offer some observations on castings in general that you may apply to these and other workings. I had considered putting these theoretical speculations and models earlier in the Castings, but I believe that you will find them more interesting now. Hopefully these closing thoughts will encourage you to re-read the various casting protocols with a fresh eye. They should also give you another frame of reference with which to consider combining different components in creating rituals.

Six Basic Modes

There are many forms and uses for castings, perhaps as many as there are magickal or religious intents and purposes. There are six modes that I believe are basic to the framing of castings in the way that the Elements are fundamental to descriptions of energy. There are many other ways to describe the modes of castings, but these are as good a starting point as any. No doubt these modes exclude some possibilities, in much the way that musical scales give order by excluding certain notes, but that is the price of any system. You may wish to experiment in creating other sets of modes to describe castings.

In practical applications castings are more often mixtures of modes rather than any one simple primary form. The following six modes are tools to describe the way that energy and information is manipulated within castings. The names for these six patterns are metaphors and as such the image suggested by each metaphor contains much of the information needed to understand the pattern.

The Vessel

In order to keep power from dissipating a casting is created to hold the energy raised in a working. Like water, energy only exhibits force and form when contained. Energy, like water, also takes on the shape of the container. To some degree almost all rituals and ceremonies use the mode of the Vessel to contain the power of the working. A special form of the Vessel is the Crucible which is meant to contain intense transformative forces. The Vessel also separates that which is within from that which is without, but its primary purpose is not protection or separation.

The Lens

The shaping and the release of magickal energy can be focused by a casting. Although this shaping and release, as in the cone of power in Wiccan magic, is often done in the mind a careful casting can refine the control of the energy. A casting can also literally shape the energy as in the Sword & Staff. It should be remembered that lenses can concentrate or diffuse energy. It should not be confused with Crucible or Vessel— the Lens actively collects and focuses whereas the Vessel merely contains.

The Fortress

For many people their first encounter with the idea of castings is the creation of protected space. This mode somewhat resembles the Vessel, but rather than holding things in the essence of this mode is keeping things out. The Fortress is clearly exemplified in the Quarters-cast circle of Ceremonial magick. A gentler form of this mode is the Sanctuary. The Fortress offers admittance to beings or energy by invitation only. The Sanctuary offers entrance to all but prohibits certain actions or energies within its bounds.

The Net

The Net selectively includes and excludes beings and energies to create a space that is a refinement of its surroundings. In some ways it has qualities of both the Lens, and the Vessel. The key idea in this mode is that the Net discriminates, discerns, and extracts specific qualities. It does not focus energy but may result in an increase in the density of energy of a specific type. Unlike some other modes, the pressures of energy/information within castings using the net mode must be equal to those of their surroundings. The Triangle of Stillness or the Star of Sight are some good examples of this mode.

The Crossroads

This mode is less common in the Western traditions but is prevalent in the Northern and Southern traditions. Castings using the Crossroads paradigm create a space that invites the Universes' participation. It's essence is the easing or encouragement of passage between planes or their union by the symbolic intersection of the qualities of the various planes. When the Quarters are treated as open gates to the Elemental Realms a Quarters-cast circle can become a Crossroads. Natural sacred sites often operate in this mode. Some forms of Druidic, Ásatrú, and Ifá rituals rely heavily on the Crossroads.

The Pantacle

This mode is named after the pantacle used in Ceremonial Magick which is usually a wax, metal, or wooden disk inscribed with symbols and glyphs. The pantacle is a schematic representation of the Magician's conception of reality. Some Wiccans refer to this as a paten, but depending upon the tradition, may or may not use it as a symbolic model of their world view. As a mode of casting, the Pantacle works with the resonance between the Microcosm and the Macrocosm with the goal of creating greater levels of congruence. As with the Vessel, this mode is a part of many ritual forms, but the Pantacle does not work by containment but rather by linkage. To use this mode as the primary mode of a ritual requires the use of a consistent and coherent magickal world view. This doesn't necessarily mean a mono-cultural ritual design, but most people find it challenging to combine cultures and systems with impunity.

The Power Of Intent

To end, I'd like to emphasize the pivotal place that intent takes in all magickal working and in castings in particular. Having your mind and will focused on a specific purpose is what sets an invocation or a symbolic gesture apart from merely reading a poem aloud or going through the motions of magick. However, there is more to intent than mind and will. Intent when used in reference to a magickal context is more than just a statement of purposes or motivations; it encompasses the full state of consciousness of the individual, their incorporated knowledge, and their karma. You are composed of many selves existing simultaneously on many levels of reality. To the measure that all those selves are united in purpose during ritual, then the actions of the ritual are repeated and broadcast upon those many levels of reality. This is how we activate and empower our rites and ceremonies.

Intent and will do not begin and end with the individual. Meditate on the full range of relationships between yourself and the Divine that are implied by the forms that your rituals take. Look to the words that you choose and to the tools that you use. Do the all the components of a ritual mean something to you? Intent is present in all the choices you may make in both the style and the substance of your magick.

Please Remember

▢   Intent is the center point of the magickal will from which all consequences arise. Seek to use these castings in a way that truly represents your intent of the moment and the intent of your life. Cause, effect, and synchronicity encountered in the realm of mundane life is quite challenging.

▢   Whatever we do in sacred space has an impact upon us that is at least three times stronger than the impact of those actions that we take in the mundane world. There is no quicker and *no steeper* a road to spiritual growth than experiences gained as a direct result or as a consequence of ritual.

I wish you safe journeys on Magick's roads.

Appendices

The following one page summaries of selected castings are not meant as substitutes for reading the chapters or for learning the castings. They are intended as quick references that you may photocopy from the book to make your rituals flow more smoothly as you work through these castings.

The appendices on the Chakras and on the Qabala are provided to give you background information and context to some of the materials presented in this book. They are woefully scant, but better than nothing.

The Sword & Staff

Casting-

By placing a Sword and a Staff at 90 degrees to each other with the Sword's point to the East and the Staff's head to the North you can generate a casting that can often be used in place of a Quarterscast Circle. Though it activates automatically in the presence of an incarnate soul, the casting builds up to a useful level faster if an invoking Pentacle is traced over the intersection of the Sword and Staff. Most other energy calling actions will also help to ignite this casting.

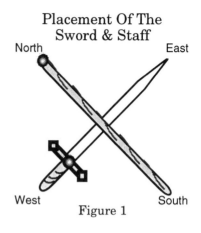

Placement Of The Sword & Staff

Figure 1

Note: The Sword and the staff should both be purified before use and ideally should be consecrated magickal tools.

Dismissal- Place the Sword and Staff parallel to each other and the energy field will dissipate faster than if they are just separated.

Description- This casting creates a continually moving double vortex, often "seen" as flames. Unlike a quarters cast circle it does not create a solid boundary, rather it is a pressure field whose energy level varies as a function of the user's focus. Control of the field is through the Element of Water the user brings to the casting.

In this casting the staff is representative of living (Raith) energy forces and of Fire. In this casting the sword is representative of non-living elemental forces and of Air. The Cross of Matter repre-

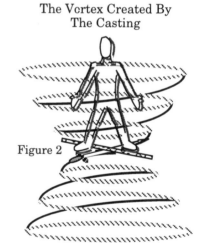

The Vortex Created By The Casting

Figure 2

sents Earth and grounds this casting. You are the Water that is the control in this casting.

Caution: Your emotional state has a great impact on the power of this casting. Never use it in anger or while experiencing volatile emotions. Do not use in combination with a Triangle of Stillness.

144

The Triangle Of Stillness

Casting-

To invoke the Triangle take crystals in the arrangement shown and send energy through them one at a time in the sequence shown. Each crystal must be charged individually with its appropriate qualities:

Point: Cardinal- the outpour, the thrust of coming into being, creation. Plus- positive polarity, pressure. The Past- the area of Causes.

Sphere: Fixed- being, preservation, balance. Minus- negative polarity, suction. The Present- the area of Formation.

Egg: Mutable- ending, returning to creation, decay, transformation. Zero- neutral polarity, agency. The Future- the area of the Unformed.

Dismissal- The Triangle is dismissed in the same sequence that it is cast. The energy should be withdrawn from each crystal and grounded out. The Triangle will take some time to fade out despite the dismissal. If there is an urgent need to return the area to its normal state you can speed up the process. After withdrawing the energy from each crystal place it in a pouch or other suitable container, so that the three are in physical contact with each other.

Description- When invoked this creates an area of stillness where causality and temporal forces are

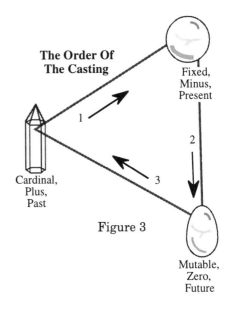

The Order Of The Casting

Fixed, Minus, Present

Cardinal, Plus, Past

Mutable, Zero, Future

Figure 3

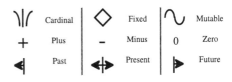

The Symbols Charged At Each Point

Figure 5

greatly diminished. This casting is useful for work involving: divination, healing, meditation, counseling, QBL work, time magic, and synchronicity.

Caution: Do not sleep or spend extended periods within a Triangle Of Stillness unless you are looking for the psychic equivalent of jet lag. Do not use in combination with a Sword & Staff casting.

The Square Of Abeyance

Casting-

1. Draw a line of matte black energy from North to South. Then one from East to West. You are in the center.

2. Create a square outlined in matte black. Starting in the N.E. fill each square in sequence with the gray energy of active neutrality*.

3. Examine the Square and make sure that every part is filled with gray energy.

4. Will away the matte black boundaries. The Square of Abeyance is complete.

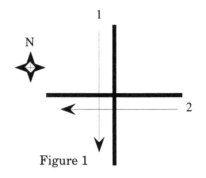

Figure 1

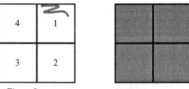

Figure 2   Figure 3

*Gray Energy: The gray energy of active neutrality is like the static of a radio or a television tuned to a missing station. It is like white or pink noise in that it contains many frequencies but in no particular pattern. It is neutral in its indecision rather than in being an average or in being indefinite.

Dismissal- The maker of the Square need only introduce into the Square a spark of energy of any bright color and the Square will fade away. With the Square of Abeyance it is possible for the maker to leave the Square after it is cast and dismiss it at a distance. This may be particularly useful if the Square was used as protection against unpleasant energies.

Description- The Square creates a space where energy patterns and frequencies that are not native to the physical plane of reality are made null and void. They

Figure 4

are held in abeyance which depending upon their nature results in stasis, dismissal, or dissolution.

Caution: Most people find being inside a Square of Abeyance feels oppressive because their psychic senses are often blocked by the Square. Many sensitives are head blind inside the Square. There is no lasting harm but it can be frightening.

The Three Pillars

Casting-

- The Externalized form of the casting requires pillars that are at least a head taller than the tallest person present.
- The Internalized form requires pillars that would fit from the bottom of the spine to the nape of the neck.
- The Microcosmically cast form uses one large set and one small set of pillars.

In the case of the internalized or the microcosmically cast forms, each individual must create their own pillars. The externalized form may be shared easily; passage through the perimeter marked by the Three Pillars does not disrupt the casting so long as energy is provided to maintain focus.

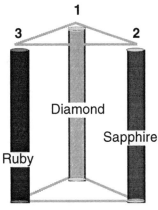

Figure 3

• Each Pillar begins with the circle of its base scribed with energy the color of the appropriate gem. Then the circle is quartered with two lines of energy forming an equal-arm cross. Another circle is scribed over the first and an invoking pentacle of earth is placed within it. If it is your custom, use the sixth sealing stroke in making the invoking pentacle. Make the circle with the star rise to the height needed for the casting. The height is determined by the form the casting will take.

• When the Pillars are complete, beginning with the Diamond Pillar, draw a veil of rainbow fire from it to Sapphire, and then to Ruby, and back to Diamond. The veil should run the complete height of each Pillar. This step in the casting may be completely

mental, but is better accomplished with gestures and motion. Rainbow fire has the transparency of a physical rainbow but with the quick, flickering, changeability of flames.

Dismissal- The pillars should be dismissed in the same order as they were cast. First, the pentacle at the top and the equal-arm cross at the bottom of the Pillar should be erased. When the equal-arm cross on the Ruby Pillar is removed, the veil of rainbow fire should thin almost to transparency. Then the Three Pillars should be seen to descend into the earth, dissolving as they do so. All the energy of the casting should be grounded. The veil of energy that enclosed the triangular shaft of the casting should be reabsorbed by the pillars, but if for any reason it seems to linger it too should be grounded into the earth.

The Star of Sight

Casting-
This technique is for 5, 7, or 9 people if there is an extra person they may stand in the center. The Circle should be scribed with violet fire, then the Star scribed in an invoking fashion. There should be a candle at each point. The candles should be purified and charged specifically for the purpose of the specific working at hand. A candle in the center if it is vacant.

Open the Transpersonal Chakra then use the Temple of Isis technique to open the Third Eye. The goal is to place everyone's transperonal chakra (personal Kether) in the center.

Dismissal- Return through the hearth and flames of the Temple of Isis. Allow the Transpersonal Chakra to close.

Then ground the Star and Circle by allowing it to dissolve into the earth.

Eat immediately after the working to close down the psychic senses. Record everyone's visions and impressions as you eat and ground.

Description- The Star of Sight is an aid to group visioning or group travel, as it encourages a blending of talents. Rather than simply comparing impressions after a group working— the Star of Sight allows for the unification of visions to increase the quality, quantity, and clarity of psychic perceptions.

Caution: The Star of Sight does not provide much protection against intrusion by unwanted influences and presences. The scribing of the circle will stop some things but it is hardly the bulwark of a Quarters-cast circle. Most of the defense is in the power of the group mind created by the casting. In most cases the strength of the group mind is a sufficient deterrent to interference. In those cases where it is not, then the role of the guardian becomes essential.

Note: Learn the Temple of Isis technique first.

The Four Minds

Casting-

Earth: Step 1

In your inner landscape look to the North. Visualize a yellow square glowing in the North. Take a breath then imagine passing through it like a portal to the realm of the Mind of Earth. Look around and attend to what you see. Then remain passive, silent and open to all impressions, especially bodily or internal sensations. When you feel prompted to move on, return through the portal of the yellow square to the plain.

Air: Step 2

In your inner landscape look to the East. Visualize a blue circle glowing in the East, then imagine passing through it like a portal into the Mind of Air. Look around and attend to what you see. The clouds, winds, and dust about you take the form of your thoughts. When you feel prompted to move on, return through the portal of the blue circle to the plain.

Fire: Step 3

In your inner landscape look to the South. Visualize a red triangle glowing in the South, then imagine passing through it like a portal into the Mind of Fire. Look around and attend to what you see. Summon your desire for the knowledge or insight that you are seeking. Concentrate on your determination to will power then return through the portal of the red triangle.

Water: Step 4

Visualize a silver crescent shining in the West, then imagine passing through it like a portal into the Mind of Water. Look around and attend to what you see. Summon your courage, your heart, and open to whatever may come. Allow all the emotions related to the question to wash over you and flow through you. Return

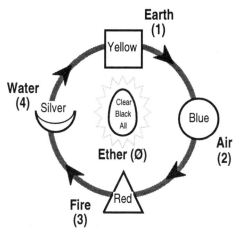

through the portal of the silver crescent to the plain and go to egg.

Ether: Step 5

Standing at the center of the plain in your inner landscape, place the egg once more in the center point of your being. Transmit to the egg all information, all the understanding, and all the answers that you gained in the Four Minds. Tell yourself that everything that you need to remember will be remembered, know that it is so. After communing with the egg, listen to see if it has any message for you.

Repeat The Cycle

Start again with the yellow square of Earth and repeat the full cycle.

Closure

At the end of a cycle, return to the egg in your center point. Recreate the state of being grounded and centered. When you feel solid place any critical pieces of information/insight into the egg.

The Chakras - The Organs Of The Subtle Bodies

What we call the aura is really our perception of our various subtle bodies. These subtle bodies interpenetrate each other and our physical body and are often identified as layers of energy or as forms that resemble the shape of the body. In terms of appearance, the Etheric body most closely approximates the shape of the Physical body. The Akashic has the greatest flexibility tends to only loosely conform to the shape of the Physical body. All of the subtle bodies are in constant motion and their forms change continually in response to the self and to the environment. In perceiving the aura this motion and flux may or may not be apparent in the same manner that the spinning blade of a propeller may seem to be a disk.

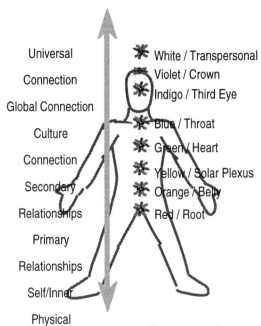

Universal Connection
Global Connection
Culture Connection
Secondary Relationships
Primary Relationships
Self/Inner
Physical

White / Transpersonal
Violet / Crown
Indigo / Third Eye
Blue / Throat
Green / Heart
Yellow / Solar Plexus
Orange / Belly
Red / Root

Chakras are the equivalent in the aura of glands and organs in the body and as such are the centers of great activity and are links between the various parts of the self. The word chakra comes from the Sanskrit word for wheel, and indeed they do resemble spinning wheels or vortices of light. We can work with the Chakras through the use of color, sound, and motion. There are many systems of which these diagrams present only one.

Note: In using sounds and colors to work with chakras keep in mind that the shift from low frequency to high frequency between the colors and/or pitches is more important than exact intervals. The locations for the chakras may vary somewhat but the sequence does not.

Chakra	Location	Color	Sound	Gland
Transpersonal	Above the head	White	Aum	All
Crown	Fontanelle	Violet	Eee	Pineal
Brow	Third Eye	Indigo	Ihh	Pituitary
Throat	Larynx	Blue	Ehh	Thyroid
Heart	Between Breasts	Green	Ahh	Thymus
Solar Plexus	Above Nave	Yellow	Aww	Adrenal
Belly	Below Navel	Orange	Ohh	Spleen
Root	Genitals	Red	Ooo	Gonads

The Qabala - The Tree Of Life

The Qabala is a diagram of the universe within and the universe without. It is like a hologram in that every piece and every place of it/on it contains information. Its major structures are:

The 10 Spheres: These are states of being

The 22 Paths: These are states of process

The Three Pillars
The Pillar Of Mercy (Force/Expansion)
The Pillar Of Severity (Form/Restriction)
The Pillar Of Mildness (Balance/Synthesis)

The Four Worlds
Atziluth: The World Of Archetypes
Briah: The World Of Creation
Yetsirah: The World Of Formation
Assiah: The World Of Manifestation

General Suggestions:

I suggest you read Dion Fortune's *Mystical Qabalah* and/or Ellen Cannon Reed's *The Goddess & The Tree* as a start. Although there are many pieces of information that are associated with each part of the Qabalah and its use, I believe that the key to understanding the Qabalah is a sense of its pattern and flow. As such I encourage you to set the books down periodically and allow yourself to daydream, brainstorm, and free-associate a bit about the material you've been studying to give yourself processing time for the non-linear component of the Qabalah work.

Ain- Nothing
Ain Sof- Infinity
Ain Sof Aur- Infinite Light

Kether — Crown
Binah — Understanding
Chockmah — Wisdom
Daath
Geburah — Might
Chesed — Mercy
Tiphareth — Beauty
Hod — Glory
Netzach — Victory
Yesod — Foundation
Malkuth — Kingdom

Basic Color Scale
(In Briah)

White
Black
Grey
Red
Blue
Yellow
Orange
Green
Violet
Ochre
Russet
Olive
Black

Exercise: Draw The Tree!

Many sources suggest that drawing the Tree and filling it in with notes, colors, and details is a useful learning tool. I agree—but in addition to that I recommend many impromptu doodlings of the Tree. The creation of a nice representation of the Tree often gets in the way of free flowing familiarity. Craftsmanship is not the goal; the goal is to make the concepts of the Tree a living part of your mental life. Create quick sketches, that take no more than a minute or two to do, several times a week. This could be a doodle on a napkin in a diner, a squiggle in the margin of a notebook, a quick scribble on a piece of waste paper that you throw away after a moments contemplation. At first you may just get the ten spheres down, maybe the paths. As you do more quick sketches challenge yourself by picking a specific category/correlation and try to depict it.

If you feel daunted by the amount of work then it probably means that you are spending too much time on each doodle. Don't be too critical of your mistakes; this is an exercise (think metaphor) to encourage flexibility, stamina, and strength.

Suggested Readings

A few titles that dovetail with the material in *Castings*.

Dolores Ashcroft-Nowicki
- *First Steps In Ritual*
- *The Ritual Magic Workbook*
- *The Shining Paths*

Paul Beyerl
- *The Master Book Of Herbalism*

Marion Zimmer Bradley
- *The Mists Of Avalon*
- *The Forest House*

Joseph Campbell
- *The Inner Reaches Of Outer Space: Metaphor As Myth And As Religion*

Sylvia Cranston
- *The Extraordinary Life & Influence Of Helena Blavatsky*

Aleister Crowley
- *Magick*
- *777*

Nevill Drury
- *Dictionary Of Mysticism And The Occult*

Janet & Stewart Farrar
- *The Witches' Way*
- *The Pagan Path* (w/ G. Bone)

Dion Fortune
- *The Mystical Qabalah*
- *Avalon Of The Heart*

Stephen W. Hawking
- *A Brief History Of Time*

Murry Hope
- *Practical Techniques Of Psychic Self-Defense*
- *The Psychology Of Ritual*

Ralph Metzner
- *Opening To Inner Light: The Transformation of Human Consciousness*

Ellen Cannon Reed
- *The Witches' Qabala: The Goddess and the Tree*
- *The Witches' Tarot*

Michael Talbot
- *The Holographic Universe*

Starhawk
- *The Spiral Dance*
- *Truth Or Dare*
- *The Fifth Sacred Thing*

Roger Zelazny
- *Nine Princes In Amber (The Amber Novels)*

About The Author

Ivo Domínguez, Jr. is a writer, an
artist, a visionary, and a practitioner of a
variety of esoteric disciplines. He has
been active in Wicca and the Neo-
Pagan community since 1978, and has
been giving workshops on Chakras,
Divination, the Qabala, Ritual, Astrology, and Herbalism since 1982. He was a
founding member, and past High Priest,
of Keepers of the Holly Chalice, the
first coven of The Assembly of the Sacred Wheel. He is now serves as an Eld-
er to the four covens of the Circle of Pisces within the Assembly.

His techniques are rooted in a syn-
thesis of traditional metaphysical teachings, modern science, and memories
from past lives. He is published regularly in a variety of Neo-Pagan publica-
tions and has other metaphysical books in the works. Ivo has been participating in sweat lodges since 1987, and has been a water pourer since 1994. He
was trained to pour by Shavierah Stonewater (Diane Duggan). He is the primary author of a Wiccan Sweat protocol that was developed by the Assembly
of the Sacred Wheel.

Ivo is an activist in a variety of movements. He served on the Wilmington
Delaware's Civil Rights Commission as its Vice-Chair and first openly gay
person. He served on the Board of the National Gay & Lesbian Task Force as
its Secretary. He was active with the Lesbian, Gay, Bisexual Student Union at
the University of Delaware, and helped to found the Gay and Lesbian Alliance of Delaware, CAMP Rehoboth, and Delaware Coalition for Lesbian,
Gay & Bisexual Rights. He was the first Executive Director of DLGHA, Delaware's primary HIV/AIDS service agency and remained in AIDS work for
nine years. He served on the State of Delaware's AIDS Advisory Task Force
and the Medical Society of Delaware's Blue Ribbon AIDS Commission. He
has been active in minority and environmental affairs in Delaware and also in
electoral politics. In the early '80s, he and his lover Jim Welch owned and
managed Hen's Teeth, Delaware's first alternative bookstore that served as a
crossroads and common ground for many communities.

He is also the author of a book of essays entitled Beneath The Skins: The
New Spirit & Politics Of The Kink Community that was published by Dae-
dalus Publishing Company of San Francisco.

You may contact Ivo at:
ivod@aol.com or panpipe@dol.net